MW01633931

Praise for *Notes from Nature*

"The *Notes* opened my heart to beauty and wonder in Nature ... helped me see beauty ... and feel awe." Chris McLeod

"*Notes from Nature* is a reminder for me to get out of my head and my tunnel vision and reconnect with nature. To slow down and to connect with what is outside of my physical space sometimes. I think it connects with me on many different levels. There is the very physical notion of getting outside and engaging, but there's also this energetic emotional connection to slowing down and listening to what nature shares through her wisdom. So, all-in-all for me, it's a reminder to be connected to what is greater than me and beyond my petty little focus which can carry me away at times." Stacy Vajta

"*Notes from Nature* got me out of my little bungalow, where I spend most of my workdays as well as my free time. Some days I literally left and walked into the beautiful mountains around me, but on days when I didn't have time to go outside, the *Notes* reminded me to stop and mentally spend some time in nature.

Overall, the *Notes* gave me a fuller sense of peace and tranquility." Peggy Shafer

"*Notes from Nature* offers snack-sized reminders to draw in your awareness, connect with yourself and nature, and to be present in your life. The personal stories shared in this book are insightful, real, and vulnerable in a way that lends comfort." Heathir McElroy, Collaborative Wellness Center

"*Notes from Nature* is a beautifully written journey of ways for all of us to connect and reconnect with nature through our whole body and mind. Angie's suggested activities help us to hear and feel all of nature's many messages to help us become more connected with our total world. Thank you for sharing your experiences and knowledge." Maureen Stoudt

Other Books Written by Angie Mattson Stegall

How Your Disorganization is Stealing Your Time, Your Attention and Your Health

Focus on Five: How to Organize Your Five Essential Business Systems ™

Ponder This: How Everyday Experiences Deliver Unexpected Insights in Business and Life

Make Some Room: Powerful Life Lessons Inspired by an Epic 16-Day Colorado River Rafting Trip Through Grand Canyon

All books are available from Amazon.com.

NOTES FROM NATURE

Tune into Your Inner Voice by Letting Nature Take the Lead

Angie Mattson Stegall

Published in the United States of America

First Edition

ISBN 978-0-578-43643-2

By: Angie Mattson Stegall
Gastonia, NC, 28054
www.AngieStegall.com

DEDICATION

This book is for everyone who has heard their inner voice while out in nature.

And for those who are willing to try.

Go to nature with your problems, your sorrows, and your prayers. Rest there until you find comfort.

Angie Mattson Stegall

Contents

INTRODUCTION

An odd thing started happening to me a few years ago: nature began communicating with me. At first it was very subtle, but when I started paying attention the communication was unmistakable. I began receiving specific messages, seeing what could only be signs meant specifically for me, and feeling a profound connection.

These moments of connection happened between me and nature when I was outside sitting, walking, kayaking, rafting, or just hanging out with another person. I found these moments of profound connection with nature helped reveal my inner voice.

As an avid writer, I recorded these events in my journal. I wrote about encounters with the rivers. With a particular rock. About fire. Even about messages I received for another person. Because these moments of connection kept happening, I started sharing them with friends on social media.

People were enthusiastic about receiving these notes from nature. I had many notes from followers confessing how much they wanted a relationship with nature but simply found it difficult to find the time to develop and nurture it. Other people told me how they used to have a deep relationship with nature, but our modern world — with our climate control, endless to-do lists, and overabundance of technological wonders — had left them feeling separated from this relationship with nature and themselves.

Reading my notes helped people reconnect. First with the natural world around them, then with themselves, their breath, bodies, feelings, sensations, and, ultimately, with their own thoughts.

This book is a compilation of the notes I've received over the years, a little bit of research (of which there is a delightfully overwhelming amount I chose not to share, but you can go find for yourself if you want it), and journal prompts I created to help my readers pay attention to and nurture their relationships with the natural world.

I hope this book will serve as gentle instructions for you to begin nurturing your own relationship with nature. I hope you will discover through time spent in nature that your inner voice reveals itself, quietly but undeniably.

Finally, I hope you will feel such a profound connection to nature that you feel called to tend it, protect it, and care even more deeply for yourself and the natural world.

The Truth

Nature longs to be in connection with you. Simply making the time to show up and be present is all it takes.

It really is that simple. However, nature's simplicity doesn't mean it is easy. It has taken years of practice — showing up, sitting, listening, and receiving — to have as many encounters as I do.

I am not special when it comes to this communicating with nature thing. I haven't been formally trained, no one (including me) has declared me to be a shaman or high priestess of nature. I wouldn't consider myself a wiccan or witch, or a medicine woman. I am simply a wayfinder (a term I learned from my mentor, Martha Beck). I am grateful to nature because through her I have found my way home.

The practices in this book can help you do this, too.

This Book as a Guide

This book is separated into three parts:

1. Body
2. Mind
3. Human/Nature Connection

In the Body section, I'll show you the path I took to reconnect with my own body and how nature assisted me. I'll provide exercises, tools, and prompts to help you get into your body and to help get your body into nature.

In the Mind section, I'll help you understand how to quiet your mind in order to ready yourself to pay attention to messages you will inevitably receive from nature. I'll also share research I've found that supports how crucial restorative breaks are for your brain and your performance and creativity.

In the Human/Nature Connection section I'll guide you to identify your own notes from nature, encourage you to spend quality time in nature, and teach you to connect deeply and profoundly with the natural world around you. I share more personal examples of my own experiences and those of my friends. Please understand that I share these not because we are different or special, I share them to show they are not all that unusual. I share them to show a range of experiences and how simple, yet profound, they can be.

Everything boils down to getting still, being open, and listening. Once you're there, be ready to receive. What will you receive? I can't say for sure. Your gift might as simple as feeling calmer. Finding a deep breath. Or it could be as transformative as an insight that answers a question you'd been wrestling with for a long time. Whatever you receive, it will be unique to you and for you. Welcome it and give thanks.

This Book as a Journal

This book is also meant to be a journal, to be carried with you. Jot your ideas, messages, and feelings on the "Journal Prompt" pages or on the extra pages at the end of each of the three sections. Throw the book in your backpack or tuck it under your arm as you head outside.

This Book as a Practice

I often go *out* to go *in* — meaning I go outside to spend quality time with my inner life. When I spend time outdoors reconnecting with my inner landscape, I discover peace and wisdom just being with the trees, the rivers, and the rocks.

In our incredibly busy world, it is anathema to suggest we slow down or (GASP!) that we *stop* when we are feeling confused, sad, out of control, or any other emotion deemed negative.

We have forgotten that we are part of the natural world. We have forgotten nature has wisdom to share with us, about us, and for us, if we would just pause long enough to connect and listen.

In the course of sharing my notes from nature, I have begun finding *so many* other people who commune with the trees, rivers, rocks, and nature as a whole. We each purposefully venture out to ask nature for guidance, instruction, and even companionship.

"Imagine a therapy that has no known side effects, is readily available, and could improve your cognitive functioning at zero cost. Such therapy has been known to philosophers, writers, and laypeople alike. [It is called] **interacting with nature."** Berman, Jonides, & Kaplan, 2008

Read this book straight through or just flip to a random entry as it calls to you. Read the entry, complete the exercise, if there is one, and spend some time reflecting with the journal prompt. This could be a very intuitive way to partner with your own true nature. This can direct you to certain parts of yourself that want to be heard and healed.

In summary, there's no wrong way to use this book.

Thanks, always, for reading. Let's get started!

Warmly,

BODY

An anxious mind cannot exist in a relaxed body.

~ Edmund Jacobson, MD

Be Present

As we begin, I'd like to ask you for one thing:

Be present right this second.

How?

Whether you're reading this lying in bed, sitting on a bus, or at your desk, my invitation is for you to be here now.

Step One: STOP (when it's safe to do so).

Step Two: Close your eyes (when you feel safe doing so).

Step Three: Feel what you're standing, sitting, or lying on. Notice what's under your feet or seat. What it feels like. Notice your hands on your phone, or on the steering wheel, or on your lap.

Step Four: Take a breath. Breathe to fill your lungs and allow your breath to move far down into your belly. Make sure you are breathing deeply enough to push your whole belly out. Relax into that pressure.

Step Five: Release the whole breath with a whooshing exhale.

Repeat. Repeat. Repeat.

All you have is right now. All that matters is this moment.

I often ask myself, "Am I comfortable? Am I safe? Am I loved?

If I can answer YES to each of the questions, then being present to the YES is all that life requires of me in this moment.

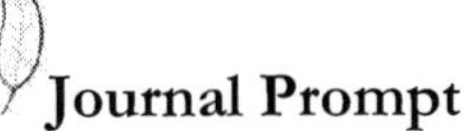

Journal Prompt

How do you feel after taking these easy, yet thoughtful, breaths? Describe your body sensations:

Breathe

From a young age, I held my breath. This habit began as an act of trying to be invisible.

As a Navy brat, each time we moved I was the new kid in school. I discovered it was safer to be invisible at first, to feel the energy of the new place, and learn the lay of the land, before revealing my presence.

I was also a swimmer throughout elementary school, and learned the three-count breath, which encouraged me to hold my breath as a discipline and practice. I was an excellent practitioner of both swimming and holding my breath.

Once, I told my mom, "I hate breathing. It's so hard."

As I got older, I became embarrassed by the sounds I made when I exercised. I was never a skinny, tiny girl. You could have described me as sturdy. Because of this, I had a bit of body dysmorphia; I *saw* myself as a fat kid. Thus, I didn't want anyone to hear me huffing and puffing. I didn't want anyone to notice me. I didn't want anyone to *look* at me. My thinking was: if I don't breathe loudly, maybe they won't notice me.

In my thirties, I attended an event that changed my outlook on breathing wholly and completely. Towards the end of the event I described my struggle with my breath to a trusted yoga teacher. He looked right at me and challenged me, *"Do you want to live?"*

That single question changed everything for me. I began to practice conscious breathing all day, every day.

The idea that breath matters for me to LIVE opened up so much for me. I realized how important my soft, animal body is. How natural breathing is. Nature wants to remind you that your breath is literally what gives you LIFE.

Do you want to live?

Yes?

Then BREATHE.

Journal Prompt

What is your relationship with your breath? Are you conscious of it? Is it a struggle? Or are you tuned into your breath in a very conscious way? Write a letter to your breath, describing your feelings about it:

Nature Is

One day as I sat outside contemplating nature, she showed me that she/he/it just IS. Here's what I was shown:

- The river just is.
- The trees just are.
- The sun, moon, and clouds all have their purpose. They don't argue with that purpose, they just are.

Do you know what is so interesting about all this?

You just ARE, too.

Somehow in life, we've gotten our worth — our very existence — all twisted up with money, titles, and what we've done or accomplished. The reality is, though, that we are just as much a part of the natural world as the rivers, trees, sun, moon, and stars. We deserve to be here just for the very fact that *we are here.*

Sit down and let that soak in for a minute.

Sometimes, when I get my knickers in a twist over finances, business, or something else I'm trying too hard to accomplish, I give up and go outside. I lie down and stare up at the sky. I think about all there is up there, beyond the clouds, the sky, the atmosphere, in the cosmos, and past the solar systems.

I start to feel very small. This gives me a much-needed reality check. And I just chill out. Lying there, I stare at the sky, taking one breath in and letting one breath out.

Taking one breath in and letting one breath out.

That small break, and that shift in perspective, brings me back to myself. Nature invites you to simply practice being who you are: a glorious part of the natural world.

> *Out beyond ideas of wrongdoing and right doing,*
> *there is a field.*
>
> *I'll meet you there.*

When the soul lies down in that grass, the world is too full to talk about. Ideas, language, even the phrase 'each other' doesn't make any sense.

~ Jalal al-Din Muhammad Rumi

I encourage you to go to that field, the one out beyond the cognitive idea of right and wrong. Lie in the grass. Breathe. Feel the sun. Breathe. Laugh with the wind.

When you are feeling centered and grounded again (back in your body, in touch with your essential self), it's time to re-enter the world. Get up. Go back to work. Be involved in your community. Love your family.

You will be different, softer, and more able to connect human-heart to human-heart. You are what the world needs to heal.

To heal the world, we must first heal ourselves. Thankfully, nature is ready and willing to help.

Journal Prompt

The next time you are feeling out-of-sorts with grief, frustration, sadness, or anger go outside. Set a timer for 10 minutes. Lie in the grass and breathe. Once the timer goes off, reflect on the changes you feel *in your body*:

Your Animal Body

Remember your body is an animal and animals aren't meant to be on guard 24/7/365.

Life is supposed to be composed of moments of awareness, occasional moments of fight or flight, but many more moments of relaxation, of being fully in the moment. For most of us modern world people, we live constantly in moments of fight and hyper-awareness/flight, but we *forget* about the *moments of relaxation* part.

Soften the animal that is your body.

To do this, find 15 minutes where you can be alone. Close the office door or go outside if the weather is nice and complete the following exercise.

Go through this rigid/relax exercise (in fancy terms Progressive Muscle Relaxation) slowly. Each flex and relax period can be as long or as brief as you like. I suggest starting with 10 seconds.

Listen to your body as you do this exercise. Remember not to over-do your rigid stretch to the point where it hurts or you cramp. For some people a five-second rigid stretch is more than adequate. Listen to your body.

Directions:

Sit or lie in a comfortable place.

Take a few deep, cleansing breaths.

Slip off your shoes and begin with your toes.

- Clench your toes and let them relax.
- Point your feet hard and let them relax.
- Roll your feet several times left and right. Relax.
- Clench your calves. Relax.
- Clench your thighs. Relax.
- Clench your buttocks. Relax.
- Tighten your lower back muscles (this can be a natural state of being for some of us). Relax.
- Pull and tighten your shoulder blades together. Relax.
- Draw in and tighten your belly/abs. Relax.

- Push your diaphragm (this is the muscle you use to breathe) out tight. Relax.
- Fill your lungs, diaphragm, and belly very full with air. Make your belly pooch out like there's a basketball in there. Relax.
- Tighten up your biceps. Relax.
- Make fists with your hands but focus on tightening your forearms. Relax.
- Make fists with your hands again. Relax.
- Tighten up your fingers. Relax.
- Draw your head forward and down until you feel tightness in your neck. Relax.
- Jut your jaw forward until you feel tension. Relax.
- Squeeze your lips together hard. Relax.
- Open your mouth wide. Stick out your tongue. Relax.
- Tighten your tongue and press it against the roof of your mouth. Relax.
- Blow 'up your cheeks with air until they are tight. Relax.
- Scrunch up your eyes tight. Relax.
- Lift your eyebrows really high. Relax.
- Wiggle your ears (if you're able). Relax.

- Move your scalp (either by flexing your eyebrows up and down or just using your hands to manipulate your scalp). Relax.

- Lie down and tighten everything up so your whole body is rigid. Relax.

- After you've gone through these steps, stay relaxed and just be for a minute to feel the blood flowing through your body.

Nature reminds you this simple relaxation practice can influence your mood for the entire day.

Journal Prompt

When do you most often notice yourself in tension (i.e. being intense)? What does it do to your breathing? What does your body feel like? How do you hold your body when you are being intense? Now, how can you soften your body in this moment?

Move Your Body

Have you ever noticed how:

- Leaves dance in the wind
- Water falls like tears
- Raindrops bounce and leap
- Trees sway
- Rocks skip across a surface
- Wolves howl at the moon
- Rabbits sit and watch
- Vines swing in the breeze
- Flowers turn their faces towards the sun

YOU are the same as the things above — the same as nature.

Connect with yourself and nature right now by going outside for a minute. Honor her with your movement as you express your emotions through dancing, crying, leaping, swaying, skipping, howling, watching, swinging, or walking. Deepen your experience by turning your face toward the warm sun, the soft moonlight, gentle wind, or warm rain.

Then remember to thank nature for providing such safe, immediate, loving guidance in this exact moment.

Journal Prompt

Investigate your feelings in this moment…

What do you want? What does your body crave? What emotion wants to be expressed?

Go Outside.

Yes, right now.

Yes, regardless of the weather.

If it's cold, put on a jacket (or don't). If it's raining, cover up with a raincoat (or don't). If it's snowing, pull on those snow boots (or don't)!

Just go outside.

Stand there.

Breathe.

Just BE outside for a few minutes.

When I think about nature, I mostly think about being outside. But when I dig a little deeper, I also think about self-care. I think of concentrating on my breathing, of being aware of my body, and about reducing my stress levels.

For example,

Hot water + my relaxing body = A Very Happy Angie

The hot water that makes me very happy can be in my tub at home, in a hot tub anywhere, or in a place like Liard Hot Springs in British Columbia — the most magnificent natural hot spring I have visited in my life. (Please take me back!)

Here is the secret of this whole book: connecting with nature is about finding ways to help you connect back to yourself. And *your* way is the right way!

Here are some suggestions for connecting yourself back to your body (circle all that apply):

Massages	Hugging trees
Meditation	Hiking
Salt caves	Kayaking
Hot springs/hot tubs	Backpacking
Sitting next to a creek	Rock climbing
Hot baths	Wing suiting
Sound therapy	Bungee Jumping
Floating	Parachuting
Yoga	Horseback riding

Bicycling   ____________(yours)
Labyrinth walking   ____________
Chanting   ____________
Singing   ____________
Dancing   ____________
Art   ____________

Significant healing happens when you stop and focus on your connection with your body and what your body wants and needs.

Nature and I invite you to find your thing and practice it with dedication, softness, and love.

Nature Does Your Body Good

I'm about to go all science geek on you, if that's okay.

The more I learn about how soil, plants, and trees help us puny humans, the more I want to tell everyone how important it is to go outside. The more I go outside, the more I want everyone to fight for the health of the trees, plants, soil, and water that support us.

In my research on forests, I learned about phytoncide compounds. Phytoncides are a collection of essential oils found in wood, plants, and some fruits and vegetables. Trees and plants emit these phytoncides to protect themselves from germs and insects.

These phytoncides don't only help trees and plants, they help us, too, when we breathe them in. In fact, studies show being in the forest affects our immune systems and the positive effects last long after we return to our homes and workplaces.

If you're feeling sick or you want to be proactive in boosting your immune system, nature encourages you to spend time with her trees and plants inhaling phytoncides.

The best part is of getting out of nature is it requires no special skills, equipment, or training. Simply go outside and inhale.

Journal Prompt

In the next few days, make a plan to spend some time with trees and plants (even an urban park or cemetery works). When you arrive, sit or wander with no effort and no plan for 20 minutes.

After your 20 minutes are up, ask yourself: do I feel differently? How does it feel to consider the idea that simply being with the trees affects my body, mind, and immune system in a positive way?

Vitamin "G"

When was the last time you walked barefoot outside? Can you remember?

More importantly, do you remember how you *felt* when you did it? Were you paying attention?

There is a practice called earthing (or grounding) that invites people to remove their shoes and walk barefoot in the dirt, sand, or grass (or on any natural substrate).

This practice allows you to ground and center yourself to the earth in a very natural way.

Studies point to an incredible number of benefits from walking barefoot on the earth, including sleeping more soundly, calming anxiety, and reducing inflammation.

Studies are also proving that our bodies interact with the electrons in the earth. The more our bodies and these electrons interact, the better it is for us. In fact, a multi-disciplinary research study by authors James L Oschman, Gaétan Chevalier and Richard Brown, published in 2015, hypothesized the interaction of our body with the earth's electrons actually makes our blood less sticky, lowers inflammation, reduces our stress hormones, and boosts our immunity.

If that sounds kind of far-out, just please stick with me here.

This may sound like a whole lot of woo-woo, mumbo-jumbo, but I would really encourage you to try earthing for yourself.

Slip your footwear off. Find some soft grass or sand and walk in small circles. Walk in bigger circles if you feel comfortable. Go for a long walk if you're feeling super brave.

I walk barefoot, a lot. Especially when I'm around sand and grass. At the beach, I have no problems being barefoot constantly. I have also walked a number of labyrinths barefooted where the ground covering was grass, sand, or teeny-tiny pebbles.

Truthfully, the experience of earthing surprised me. Slipping my shoes off to stand on the earth, planting my feet firmly, and noticing the sensations was a new experience in full awareness. And I found each time I practiced, the rush of endorphins I experienced was incredible. Energy bubbled up through my body and rushed out the top of my head. I felt myself breathing with purpose, walking with purpose, and feeling my whole body respond.

I tried earth-walking again when I was in Joshua Tree National Park in the fall of 2017. My husband and I were hiking on a well-marked trail and I walked at least a quarter of a mile barefoot. Again, that rush of endorphins at the end was wild.

Don't believe me? That's okay. I invite you to try some Vitamin "G" for yourself. Practice earthing the next time you see a particularly lovely bit of green grass or sand. Pay attention to how you feel before and after. You might just be surprised at the difference.

Journal Prompt

Earthing exercise:

Slip off your shoes and socks. Stand and feel the earth under your feet. Wiggle your toes. Rock back and forth.

Walk in a small circle. Walk a bit further. Challenge yourself to walk a mile without shoes on natural ground.

Pay attention to how you FEEL before, during, and after.

Record your experience on the next page — and the differences you observe:

Posture Matters

There's this thing I do when I'm sitting. I didn't realize I was doing it until a friend was sitting across from me and pointed it out.

She said, "Do you know you're sitting there with your shoulders hunched up to your ears?"

I immediately dropped my shoulders and said, "Nope, I didn't realize I was doing that."

I took a few deep breaths, did a few shoulder rolls, and I've been attempting to stop being in this stress posture ever since (for a couple of years, at least).

Why do I sit like this? When did I learn to hunch my shoulders up? This is a mystery to me, still.

I can tell you that awareness helps. Meditation also helps. Yoga really, really helps.

When I was regularly receiving body work (practices called Network Spinal Analysis, which is a type of chiropractic energy healing, as well as Somatic Respiratory Integration, and Body Wisdom Therapy, I healed my lower back. I radically improved my posture. Even my breathing was a million times better.

And my body remembers that healing — I can move this way and that and feel the popping and loosening. Yet, it is a practice. One I have to be very persistent with.

The practice and attention are worth it, though, to have a healthier, better-aligned body. It's no fun to go through life with my shoulders scrunched up around my ears. I might as well be wearing a sign that announces, "I'm stressed!"

Instead, I'd like to go through life relaxed and well oxygenated. It's so much healthier and more natural.

Will you join me in relaxing your shoulders and your back?

Take three big, deep breaths, the kind of breaths where you breathe in so deeply it makes your belly poke out.

Relax and breathe. Relax and breathe. Relax and breathe.

52

Feel better?

I do!

Journal Prompt

Right now, notice your posture. Are you in tension or relaxed? Write what you're thinking about.

Can you soften your stance? Invite deeper breathing. Stretch. Yawn.

Describe what's different after breathing and stretching.

Your Toes are a Miracle (really, they are!)

I have a serious question for you: have you ever sat and just looked at your toes?

For the majority of us humans, we've got ten. Did you know some cats have more than ten toes and they are called polydactyl?

But back to your human toes...

Have you really spent time looking at them?

(NOTE: If toes gross you out for some reason, look at your fingers. They are a miracle, too!)

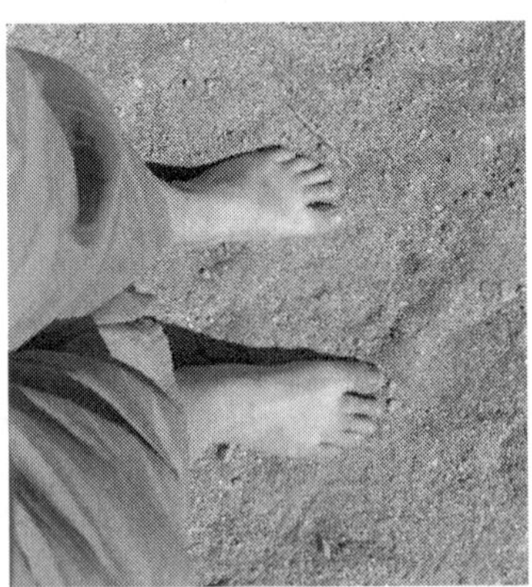

Without judging, just look. Observe their color. Their shape. Their bend-i-ness. Their nails. Their knuckles. Remember, your body is part of nature and deserves to be honored as much as the water and trees and sun.

Take a moment right this second to notice your toes for the balance and support they provide to your body and for bearing your weight when you walk. Thank them for the service they do for you by honoring them just for a minute.

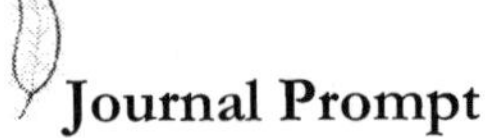 **Journal Prompt**

If you've never really looked at your toes, take a minute and do it. Set a timer and just be aware of them.

Write a Thank You note to your toes.

Get Moving

I struggle to get enough exercise. My mind believes exercising for the sake of exercising seems onerous and boring. I'd rather be curled up in a chair with an excellent book or pecking away at my computer expelling the build-up of words from my brain.

But put me on a hiking trail and suddenly I have a reason for moving this bod (which I say is built for comfort, not speed). Send me off in a kayak and I'll paddle a full day and 20 miles with a smile on my face.

Regarding this exercise thing, though, one night a few years ago, something small shifted in my brain.

I was out, around 10pm, walking my cat. I should explain that my cat, Hobbes, used to be a free-range cat and came and went through the swinging dog door at will. Since my husband and I decided to sell everything we own and live, work, and travel full-time in our motorhome (since 2017), I just don't feel comfortable sending Hobbes out the door into strange places unsupervised. So, now we go for walks, with him in a harness and me holding the leash.

On this particular night, we were walking around a big field in Flagstaff, Arizona. The night was very cold — in the 20's — and I was bundled up in a jacket with my hood up. The sky was clear, and the stars were amazingly bright.

Hobbes had his red harness on and we walked around the field and up the driveway several times. He was so happy to get out and stretch his legs, sniffing the ground, breathing the cold air, and getting quite excited when he spotted a small bird fluttering around in the brambles.

Walking around in the crisp cold night air, I realized I was moving my body and it felt really good. Hobbes was moving his body and it felt really good to him, too. Together, we were doing a form of exercise, albeit gentle and in no way aerobic. But that didn't matter because we were out there moving.

I realized that when I think of exercising, I think of sweating, breathing hard, and running on treadmills (or "dreadmills" as my friend Kenny calls them) at the gym.

Bleh.

That night, the night sky and crisp air reminded me exercise doesn't have to be like that. Gentle movement does a body good, too!

Journal Prompt

When was the last time you gave your body some gentle movement? Stretching, strolling, and wandering all count. Good for the mind, body, and soul (and good for the cat, too). What gentle movement does your body crave right now? Honor your body by doing that movement right now. Write about what is different after you've moved:

Nature is Your Body — Your Body is Nature

The mountains are my bones
The rivers my veins
The forests are my thoughts
And the stars are my dreams
The ocean is my heart
Its pounding is my pulse
The songs of the earth write
The music of my soul
       — Unknown

THIS. If there is a secret, it is what's written in the poem above.

If there is a key to unlock everything, it is this. And if there's a passcode, you'll find it here.

In order to connect to yourself, simply connect back to nature — of course, this is only my opinion, but it's shared by lots of folks, both modern and ancient.

Nature says, "I'm whispering in your ear. Are you listening?"

Nature says, "The answers are found in your pulse. Can you feel them?"

Nature says, "There's music in you. Come join me to find it."

Hearing my own inner voice whisper in the silence of nature is the hardest thing I've ever done. My inner voice is so quiet. So shy. So elusive.

And I don't have it all figured out. I still don't always make time to go out and just sit. I don't always make time for the walks, hikes, and kayaking journeys that refill me.

It's a practice. Let's journey into nature together to discover our true inner voices.

Additional Thoughts

Additional Thoughts

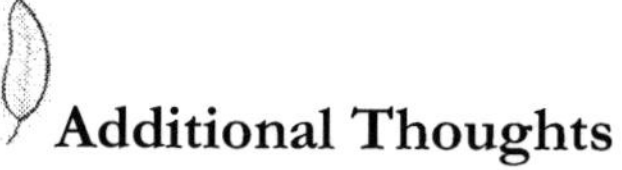 **Additional Thoughts**

Additional Thoughts

MIND

And into the forest I go, to lose my mind and find my soul.
- John Muir

This section on the mind exists to help you get *out* of your mind.

It will be important that you get into your body (see earlier section), out of your mind (this section), and connecting with nature in order to begin hearing your inner voice. This time spent in nature can be five minutes, five hours, or five days. Trust nature to take the lead. And trust yourself to receive.

Studies are clear that we have evolved to live in a fight/flight state of mind. Animals live the same way, with one important difference: when animals are not in fight mode or flight mode, they are in rest mode. We discussed this earlier.

Our modern lives are simply not set up for us to settle into rest mode for long. Part of this is due to the endless news cycles telling us how horrible and dangerous the world is, the endless YouTube videos *showing* us how horrible and dangerous the world is, and our imaginations, which can fill in how horrible and dangerous the world is based on what we've seen and heard. We are also constantly stimulated by lights, sounds, objects, and technology in our indoor *and* outdoor environments.

Florence Williams, in her book *The Nature Fix*, explains that our eyesight evolved to view large, less-complicated landscapes. However, today's modern world is crammed with buildings, houses, automobiles, flashing lights, billboards, signs, and other people talking, moving, and distracting us. This endless stimulation of our frontal cortex is exhausting to our brains.

There's a different way to get out of your mind. It's easy, healthy, and free.

Get out into nature.

Mind Your Mind

You have a sacred inner landscape that makes up your interior life. This sacred inner landscape is created by your experiences, feelings, beliefs, thoughts, and opinions.

You alone are responsible for the health and care of your sacred inner landscape. This place, when you first discover it, could be full of what I would describe as weeds, thorns, and invasive species. Things that are sharp and potentially painful. Or broad and remove all light. Or thick and push out all the others. These live in your mind. The weeds, thorns, and invasive species are metaphors for limiting thoughts and negative beliefs about yourself and your place in the world.

- I am not good enough.
- I am not lovable.
- I have to do things perfectly or people will get mad at me.
- I'm not creative.
- I'll sound stupid.
- I'm alone and that is a bad thing.
- I'm not smart enough.

- I'm not pretty/handsome enough.
- I am not rich enough.
- I'm not successful enough.
- I am not thin enough.

You did not consciously plant these metaphorical weeds, thorns, or invasive species in your inner landscape. Some were planted by you as you learned life lessons from family members and friends. Some were planted by authority figures out there in the world (think school, church, community). Some blew in on the wind of clever advertisements created by marketing strategists.

And there are also wonderful things to be found in your inner landscape: beautiful trees, happy shrubs, glorious flowers, and whimsical mosses. Consider those things metaphors for loving thoughts and powerful beliefs about yourself and your place in the world:

- I am lovable.
- I am perfect just the way I am.
- I have a great sense of humor.
- I belong.
- I matter.

- I am part of something bigger than myself.
- I am successful (and I get to define what "successful" means for me).
- My body is perfect just the way it is.
- I am beautiful inside and out.
- I am rich in so many ways.
- I am smart, clever, and creative.

Interestingly, many of these things were also planted by family members, friends, authority figures, or religious institutions, marketing strategists, etc.

As an adult, it is now your responsibility to explore your inner landscape. To make a regular habit of examining what's there by digging deep and seeing what you uncover.

The good news is *you* get to decide what stays and what has to go from your sacred inner landscape. This means you get to gently pull out anything that doesn't serve you. And you get to plant more of the things you love, including positive thoughts and joyful beliefs.

Spend as much time as you can tending to your inner landscape. Make it a priority to weed, water, and plant new, empowering thoughts regularly. Nurture this part of yourself and you'll see the metaphorical fruits of your labor spill out into other areas of your life. Those positive habits (the beliefs and thoughts you've carefully tended) will ripple out to affect your family, your community, and, eventually, the world, in wonderfully healing ways.

Interestingly, I found as I began paying attention to the inner landscape of my own life, it dawned on me how fully connected nature wants to be with me!

I discovered spending time in nature — reflecting, receiving messages, and finding the way home to my true nature — is what allowed me to become aware of what was in my inner landscape. I have suggested an exercise below to help you get started exploring and tending *your* inner landscape.

First, something important: because it is *my* responsibility to remove the things I don't want in my own inner landscape, I can get rid of certain weeds and invasive species and/or just prune or cut back the shrubs and trees. Some things are just old and overgrown, and it is time simply to trim the excess. Some things, though, need to be pulled out completely, roots and all. I do this gently, with care and compassion. I don't want to rip anything out in anger or frustration, lest I accidentally leave pieces of the roots that still have a hold and will continue grow stronger. I also don't want to leave seeds that might re-emerge later. Anything unworthy of my sacred inner landscape has got to go!

Here's an exercise to begin examining the inner landscape of your life: Sit quietly (preferably outside where you feel safe and won't be disturbed). Ground and center yourself with your breath. Sit firmly on your butt. Breathe again. Allow your thoughts to wander.

Notice the feel-good thoughts that show up. Examples: *I like myself. I am loved. I feel so connected to my family. My community is so loving. I adore my dog.* Those are the ones to nurture, fertilize, and encourage. Plant more of those!

Next, note the ones that don't feel good. Examples: *I hate myself. I'm a failure. Nobody loves me. Life is hard.* These are the thoughts that are begging to be pulled out, gently and with compassion. Make sure you pull the roots and don't leave any leftover seeds. In their places, go back and plant more good thoughts. Examples: *I love myself. I am worthy. Many people love me.*

Life is good. Nurture those thoughts daily by saying them out loud and finding one sincere example for each of them each day. Write them down as a practice of daily gratitude each day for 21 days.

Next, there are some thoughts that simply need pruning. They've run amok but a little trimming will turn them around. For example: *I am a jerk when I am driving* could be pruned to *when I am driving, I practice patience.* Another example: *I am not creative at all* could be pruned to *I am creative when I'm working on X.* Describe X in detail. Write this down and practice saying this as a gratitude statement each day for 21 days.

Repeat this exercise often until your inner landscape is full of joy, love, and abundance.

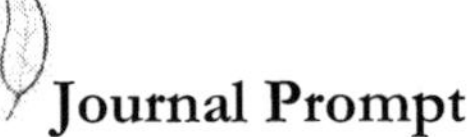

Journal Prompt

Use these pages to write down what stays and what goes from your internal landscape.

Positive, helpful, nurturing thoughts:

Use these pages to write down what stays and what goes from your internal landscape.

Yucky, unkind, unwanted thoughts:

Use these pages to write down what stays and what goes from your internal landscape.

New, loving, positive thoughts (be specific!)

Looking Versus Seeing

You can look out a window and see nothing.

Sometimes I sit in the grass near a creek or under a tree. I'll start looking at a three-by-three-inch piece of ground in front of me. At first when I'm looking, it may appear that nothing is happening.

But as I look longer, I begin to *see*.

Small insects moving around.

Bits of dirt, rock, and moss.

Sometimes I'll see bits of plastic or other trash.

Every once in awhile a bird will fly nearby or my cat will
show up and flop down in front of me. Then *he* becomes part of what I see.

Nature gently reminds you there is value in focusing on what is in front of you, not for any other reason than to just see what is there (and there's ALWAYS something there).

Exercise: Go outside. Choose a spot to sit. Maybe a tree beckons you to sit under her leaves and branches. Maybe a stream calls out for your company. Or maybe the grass is whispering in your ear. Whichever you choose, settle in and look down. Inspect what is right in front of you. Spend 10 minutes just looking.

Write about what you see and how you feel, even if you feel a little silly sitting there. Write about how your body and breath feel sitting there, just looking.

Journal Prompt

After you sit for the 10-minute exercise above, ask yourself, "What do I want *right now*?"

No judgment. Just a simple, honest answer:

Find Your Stillness

Let's practice something deceptively simple: finding your stillness.

I took the photo you see below one fall day when I was out hiking in the Coconino National Forest near Flagstaff, Arizona.

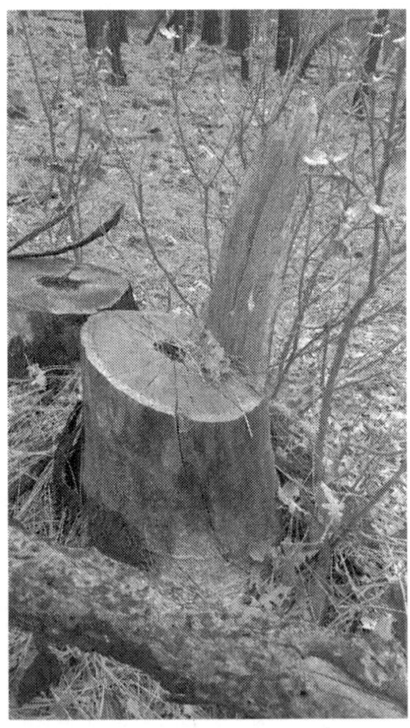

After crashing around in the woods and having a great time I stumbled across this miracle: a tree stump that looked to me like a chair.
This tree stump invited me to sit and stay awhile.

So I did.

And after a few deep breaths, I discovered a lovely inner stillness.

You don't need to go somewhere deep into the forest to find your own stillness. Your porch or back steps will do the trick.

Go. Sit. Find your breath. In doing that, you'll find the stillness. Take a few healing deep breaths and enjoy it.

Journal Prompt

Why do you resist sitting and staying awhile? What judgments do you have about sitting and doing nothing? Explore them here:

Watching the Sun Rise

There's something magical about getting up before dawn.

There is a special kind of stillness. A quiet that is like a private moment before the whole world starts to whirl and swirl with its busyness.

I love it ... and I hate it.

My perfect waking time is somewhere around 7am. No alarms to jolt me awake with a gasp, a groan, and a pounding heart.

And yet...

The pre-dawn is so beautiful. And it holds an invitation.

The mystic poet Rumi says it best:

> *The breezes at dawn have secrets to tell you*
> *Don't go back to sleep!*
> *You must ask for what you really want.*
> *Don't go back to sleep!*

People are going back and forth
across the doorsill where the two worlds touch,
The door is round and open
Don't go back to sleep!

Journal Prompt

What secrets does the waking time have to share with
you? If you must ask for what you really want, what is
it? Write it down, right now, before you lose your
nerve.

Stop and Breathe

One day, nature came to me with a message:

"Stop for a minute. Be here now. Pet me."

Pet me?

Yes — pet me.

I have the sweetest, cuddliest, most awesome-est orange cat named Hobbes.

He frequently delivers notes from nature to me in the form of asking me to be here now — to be totally present with him.

Even as I type this, he's laid himself across my hands in an effort to coax me to stop, pay attention to him, and give him generous amounts of pets and belly rubs.

Journal Prompt

Pay attention to those times when nature, in whatever form, asks you to stop and be present to the moment you're in. So, stop.

What is asking for attention right now?

Shinrin-Yoku

At the end of October, I took a client out to the woods to do some forest bathing with me.

The Japanese practice of forest bathing is formally called Shinrin-Yoku and is all about being in the presence of the trees and out in nature. Beginning in the 1980's in Japan, this practice was critically important for a working population who were literally dropping dead at their workplaces because of the stress of their work culture.

Shinrin-Yoku caught on in the USA because our levels of stress have risen, too. Between budget cuts, technology, and shrinking workforces, many people are being asked to do much more with much less.

I've found forest bathing a very powerful practice for myself and have started offering it to my clients who are interested in trying a slightly different, but very powerful, form of self-leadership and inner wisdom coaching.

On this particular day, although it was nearly November, the sun was out, and the temperature was quite warm.

As my forest bathing client and I started up a second trail for part-two of her Shinrin-Yoku experience, my instructions to her were to listen. "Listen to what's around you. Listen to what's not there. Listen to what's in here." I pointed to her heart.

She set off on her journey.

As I started to follow along behind her, nature said to me, "Take your shoes off."

I hesitated. This forest walk was not about me. I needed to be present and available for my client.

"Take your shoes off," nature said again.

"Ummmm," I thought to myself, "who knows what's on this trail. There could be glass or nails or...or...or...animal poop!"

"Take your shoes off," nature said again (for she can be quite patiently persistent with me).

So, I did as she asked and slipped off my shoes and socks. The ground was cool but dry. I wiggled my toes. And I began walking.

Ouch ouch ouch ouch ouch ouch ouch.

Every step was an effort. Sharp rock here, pointy stick there, shifting sand that moves my foot into the side of yet another sharp rock over there.

"Slow down," nature suggested.

So, I did. I began to pay exquisite attention to where and how I placed my foot down. I began looking for the right place to land my foot. A flat rock. A sandy patch. Or even a deep leafy area.

First left, then right.

First heel, then ball, followed by toes.

I started to fall into a rhythm, while still walking sooooo slowly and carefully. Suddenly, I felt the ground in a different, more intimate way. I started seeing where to put my foot before even placing it down.

Soon, nature and I were having a bit of dance. A slow dance, but still a dance. My confidence grew, so much so that when I walked up to the small creek, I decided to cross it barefooted.

The water was cool as I placed each foot deliberately on each rock, finding my way across. I felt such a victory when I reached the other side. And I felt ... different. Connected. Changed.

It was a powerful experience to slip off my shoes and really feel earth under my feet. To walk with nature, connect with nature, in a way that I hadn't in a long time.

I'd done plenty of barefoot walking on grass and at the beach. Sand and grass are easy and generally barefoot friendly. But walking barefoot in the forest?   That was a first for me, probably since I was a little kid.

I can happily say I'll be doing a LOT more barefooted forest bathing.

Journal Prompt

Forest bathing, at its essence, is about being present to what is, right now. Close your eyes, take a deep breath. Use your SIX senses and be present to what is.

What do you…

Feel:

Taste:

Touch:

See:

Hear:

Sense:

Bring Nature Inside

Way before Christmas (or even the idea of Christianity) became a thing, people were drawn to plants and trees that stayed green all winter. They were special because looking at the greenery reminded people that spring would come again.

This was especially important as the beginning of winter set in and daylight hours were in short supply — that magical winter solstice.

The winter solstice is the shortest day and longest night of the year in the Northern hemisphere (usually December 21st or 22nd). The story of the solstice began with ancient civilizations who worshipped a sun god. When darkness arrived, these people believed their sun god was suffering from sickness and weakness. The solstice became the time when the sun god returned to health. People brought evergreen boughs into their homes to remind them of the time when the plants would again be green, and the sun god would return healthy and strong.

There's something to be said for having a visual reminder that summer will come again, especially when we are experiencing winter's cold grip.

I tend to not get morose and depressed until sometime mid-February. It's then that I'm cursing the cold and the dark.

But December? No.

In December, it's my tradition to make my way to a farm in the mountains of North Carolina and pick out a little tree. My husband and I chop it down, cart it home, cover it in colored lights, and hang ornaments from the branches. For me, there's something ridiculously magical about having a tree inside my house.

I like to sit in my living room in the dark and turn on the colored strings of lights. Sometimes I play music, but often I just want to sit in my jammies, wrapped in my favorite red blanket, while staring at the lights adorning the tree in my house where it is warm and cozy.

I love bringing nature inside. Yes, yes, I understand I've killed the tree by chopping it down, but I'll put it use in a New Year's Eve bonfire or sink it in the lake to use as a fish habitat.

But I digress ...

I love bringing nature inside this time of year — or any time.

Throughout the year I collect shells, or tiny pine-cones, or I may pick up a rock that speaks to me. I'll create a little altar by my desk just to enjoy looking at the natural pieces.

Nature wants to remind you: bring her indoors, too. House plants, holiday trees, fresh-cut flowers, and even tiny mementos where you'll see them — they all count.

Journal Prompt

What have you brought inside from nature? Take a walk around your house and identify the items.

Why did you choose them? Why do they matter to you? How do they make you feel when you look at them?

If you don't have anything, can you head out and find something? It doesn't have to stay there forever. Just for today, bring something of nature inside.

Love is My Religion

Nature reminds me that love is my religion. Nature reminds me many of my close friends talk about going to church and then head out skiing, or to their kayaks, or strap on hiking boots.

Even right now as I write this, I can feel nature giggling with glee right outside the window. She loves that people go out to enjoy her and she loves that they feel more peaceful and connected when they are with her.

Nature wants me to remind you that you are free to choose that which delights you. That which builds you up.
And that which fills you.

Today — and everyday.

Journal Prompt

What is your religion? How do you practice it? What threads of nature can be found there?

Wait (something is always happening)

During the summer of 2016, my husband Nelson and I went on an epic 6,000-mile road trip to visit Glacier National Park, Yellowstone National Park, Devil's Tower National Monument, and the Badlands in South Dakota.

We had a glorious time!

And, there's one particular afternoon that stands out for me above all others.

We were in Glacier National Park at a remote campground called Bowman Lake. Late that afternoon, as we sat in camp, we could feel the wind change. We could see clouds gathering in the distance. Nelson smiled, grabbed his camera, and said, "Let's go down to the lake to take some photos."

And so we did, carrying our folding camp chairs and beverages for the short walk to the lakeside. We settled down in our chairs. Nelson started snapping photos. I was probably reading a book or staring off across the lake contemplating life.

Suddenly the wind burst from its shelter, the waves rolling along the lake surface, and the clouds began speeding in. People around us were gathering their stuff and hurrying back to their campers. Kayakers were racing across the lake, trying to make it back to shore before the wind and waves overtook them. Then there were only a few of us left, gaping at the approaching storm.

The clouds kept building as the storm sped across the lake. Soon, though, it was clear that the worst of the wind and rain would miss us. And just as suddenly, the storm passed. As it did, the most beautiful rainbow appeared over the mountains.

In that moment, nature reminded me that at the end of the rainstorm there's often a rainbow. But the more important message that day was *wait and see what happens.*

If we had been unwilling to watch the storm, if we had chickened out and left when the raindrops started pelting us, we would have missed the glorious ending with the rainbow.

Journal Prompt

This one comes directly from nature: where can you stick it out longer and risk just a little more in order to see what happens? Ignore what your brain is telling you. Wait and see what happens.

Recall a time where your patience was rewarded with something amazing:

The Mind Versus Nature

The mind likes complexity. Your true nature likes simplicity.

The mind lives for noise, confusion, ego, and busyness all the time.

Nature prefers exquisite clarity, calm, and quiet, except when something else is needed in the moment.

The problem, at least for me, is moving from that never-ending harried state of mind into my heart, where clarity, calm, and quiet live.

The single best way for me to shift my energy is to step away from my technology (phone, computer, television, etc.) and go out for a long hike. Or get in my kayak and engage in a moving mediation. Or even to sing and dance.

Nature wonders why you aren't spending more time with her. She's curious why you're feeling addicted to the noise, confusion, ego, and busyness all the time.

Nature invites you to join her more often, not to do anything specific, but rather to just be with her.

Settling into the calm, quiet, and clarity can be hard at first.

We are very used to the go-go-go and it's hard to sit and be still. When you sit still, how do you feel? Anxious? Frustrated? Guilty? What feelings bubble up the longer you sit? Do you feel compelled to do something while you're there? Do you find yourself up and wandering, often without even realizing right away you're up and wandering? This exercise in noticing is the right place to start.

When anxiety or frustration or guilt or other judgment comes up, great! Embrace each feeling. Notice it. Send it love.

Say to yourself, "I love that I feel anxious. It means I'm awake. I love that I feel frustrated. It shows me where I can grow. I love that I feel guilt. It's a part of me worth noticing."

Journal Prompt

Nature loves everything about you. What would it feel like for you to do the same?

Resilience

I'm a bit of a geek when it comes to the study of the human brain and why we act the way we do. I'm particularly a fan of articles in the *Harvard Business Review*, which combine a lot of psychology of behavior with some great business (and life) advice.

A book review I read recently really got me thinking. World-famous speaker and author of *The Happiness Advantage*, Shawn Achor, dissects the key to mental toughness — and it isn't what you think.

He explains, **"Resilience is how you recharge, not how you endure."**

What?

Go read that again.

"Resilience is how you recharge, not how you endure."

Resilience is how you recharge.

Resilience is not how you endure.

Resilience is NOT about enduring.

Resilience is about RECHARGING.

Most people seem to think that mental toughness is about endurance. Most people think that working harder leads to better work. Most people think you need resilience to keep going.

Turns out, studies prove that *recharging* is what builds your resilience. Recharging is the super power that allows you to keep going.

Think of it this way — the more charge you have in your battery, the longer and stronger you can go.

And it's worth saying that your batteries need recharging regularly. Just like watches need winding. And ponds need refilling. Oceans need tides — and waxing and waning moons to accomplish those tides. Animals need times of rest and sleep. So do humans!

Imagine that.

Here's where nature gets all excited: She invites you, anytime, to recharge with her. Build your resilience with her help! Disconnect from the whirlwind of life for a moment, a minute, an hour, or several days, in order to recharge yourself.

Rest. Rest. Rest. In doing this, nature helps you build up your resilience bank, so you can endure life. It's worth noting that to endure as a verb means to continue to exist. So, if you want to continue to exist, you must refill and recharge.

It is also worth noting that the definition of retreat is a break from extremes. Our modern life can be an exercise in managing the extremes. Give yourself the gift of restoration by retreating into nature to build up your resilience.

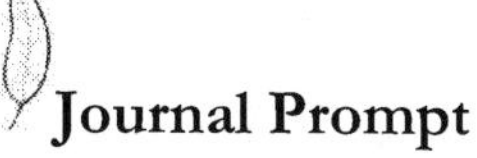

Journal Prompt

When you think of recharging, what ideas come to mind? List them all here (and then choose one to practice joyfully).

Additional Thoughts

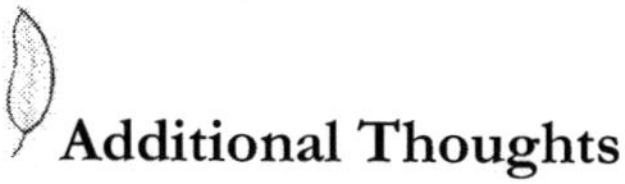

Additional Thoughts

Additional Thoughts

Additional Thoughts

HUMAN/NATURE CONNECTION

The snow goose need not bathe to make itself white. Neither need you do anything but be yourself.

Lao Tzu

Nature is Always Communicating

Nature shared a message with me when I was out watching the sunset with my husband, Nelson, recently.

We parked our car at one of the turnoffs on the Blue Ridge Parkway near our home. As is his way, Nelson set up his camera and started shooting photos.

As is my way, I started tromping around to see what I could see. I saw the normal stuff — trash left by humans, birds in trees singing an evening song, and all kinds of trees and plants and rocks.

As I ventured a little further down the hill, I saw this (see photo next page) and immediately felt my heart swell.

I called Nelson over and said, "Will you look at that! Nature is glad we're here and is sending us a message of connection and love."

Now, you could scoff at me and reply, "Well, anyone who goes there could see that sawed-off tree stump."

And my reply to you would be, "Sure, but many people wouldn't take the time to look. And if they were just aimlessly wandering around, they might not see or receive what I saw and understood."

It's a beautiful and sacred practice to allow messages like this one into your awareness. Into your life.

Gentle reader: nature is always in communication with you. Are you listening? Are you seeing? Are you paying attention?

Journal Prompt

If you'd like, ask to receive a message from nature today. Ask for one specifically just for you. Then, go about your day. Once you receive it, come back and write here about this message of connection from nature.

Receiving

My friend Sandra Trca-Black is a fellow wayfinder, which means she's also been trained by Martha Beck on how to go wordless and drop into oneness (see the Appendix for book recommendations by Martha Beck that go into great detail on wordlessness and oneness).

Sandra has made some *big* moves in her life over the past few years. Scary big. The details are hers to tell, but when she shared on Facebook about a message she received from the Pacific Ocean, it felt like a message we all could benefit from hearing. The ocean gave her permission to share it publicly and she gave me permission to share it with you here in this book.

The ocean shared:

"Go now, live your life. I was here for you when you needed me. I'll be here if you need me again. You brought your family to meet me. Your son found his spirit in my waves. I gave you hope and a vision and you acted on it. You did that. You did so much with what I gave you. I send you on now with grace and blessings, with hope and a new vision. You choose to be a surfer. You check the tides. You show up ready.

You read the waves. You fall. You get back up again. You keep showing up. When you're tired, be a sea otter. Find a safe place. Take float. Worry not about the waves. You will be held safely until it is time to surf again. You are meant for the bluffs, the water, the energy of the waves. You'll fall and get soaked sometimes, of course, but you'll be far happier than if you choose to stay on the walkway."

This message came to Sandra not as she was begging for an answer, but after she'd followed the prompts, signs, and instructions that it was time for her (and family) to make some radical moves.

Sitting in wordlessness and oneness with the ocean, she was given the gift of acknowledgement. The gift of knowing she was on the path to her right life.

Communion with the natural world — and especially with an ocean — is a gift one does not soon forget.

Journal Prompt

Sometimes, the act of sitting next to a tree, rock, river, or ocean is an invitation in itself. Go. Sit. Listen without expectation. Breathe. Be prepared to receive a feeling, a vision, a word, or a message.

What did you receive?

Cultivating Magic

"If waking up is the goal, bewilderment is the method."
Martha Beck

I'm interested in magic. Not the kind of magic with cauldrons, pointy hats, and warts of toads, though, but the kind of magic that is natural and healing. This natural and healing magic happens when I tune in, listen, and act from a place of being centered and grounded.

So, it was a huge pleasure and surprise to read Martha Beck's newest book (a work of fiction, no less!) called *Diana, Herself: An Allegory of Awakening*. Delightfully, it's going to be a trilogy, so there are two more books I'm eagerly anticipating.

Diana, Herself is about magic. Natural magic. Martha writes, "If waking up is the goal, bewilderment is the method."

I am a word nerd, so bear with me here. Martha's use of the word bewilderment stuck with me. In this magical book, Martha describes the seven tasks of bewilderment. And they are literally instructions to help you. Are you ready?

BE WILDER in order to help you get back to your TRUE NATURE.

I get so tickled thinking that the solution to what ails me — the thing I'm bewildered by — can be solved by simply going out and BEING WILDER.

HA!

And you might know this, too, if you have bit of magic in your own bones.

Let me ask you:

Do you solve problems by going for walks?

Does inspiration come to you while you're in the shower?

Does staring out into the nothingness of an expansive view give you perspective?

Does sleeping outside cure everything that ails you?

Is gardening a moving meditation for you?

Do the trees, rocks, and rivers speak to you?

Nature wants you to embrace your true nature and go be wilder every single day.

Journal Prompt

What activities bring you home to yourself? What actions help you solve problems? And finally, what makes you feel grounded and alive? Note those things here. And, go BE WILD while doing more of them!

Broken Open

A couple of years ago, I listened to a book on Audible.com called *Marrow* by Elizabeth Lesser. In this book, the author shares her journey of her sister's bone cancer. The book is a full of wisdom, sorrow, joy, and love.

Throughout the book the author's sister shares her thoughts, too. Many of them center around gardening, plants, and her love of the natural world.

They both speak often of being broken open.

When they speak of being broken open, I think of spring. Spring is a season of being broken open. Of starting new things.

We break the soil up after a long winter to ready it for spring. We poke a hole in the soil to deposit a seed. We tamp the soil back down to protect the seed.

That seed breaks open and pushes up, up, up. Soon, the seed breaks the soil again as a new shoot emerges. The new plant will break and produce a bud. That bud might produce new leaves, or seeds, or a bloom.

And it isn't always easy, this act of breaking open. But it IS natural. It IS nature's way. And WE are nature, through and through.

Poet, ordained Buddhist Monk, and songwriter Leonard Cohen said it best when he shared that the cracks are how the light gets in.

If you are feeling cracked or broken, nature asks you to take heart — without those cracks, no light could get in. No growth could take place. Those cracks open us up to SEE.

 **Journal Prompt**

In what areas of your life are you feeling broken?

In what areas of your life are you ready to be broken open?

If you are broken open, what happens when the light gets in?

An Invitation

When I was 23 or 24, a boyfriend and I were lying in the grass together staring up at the blue sky. We were young and very much in love.

As the warm breeze blew across our faces and bodies, I felt the winds of change coming. I looked at this man and said, "Can you hear the grass talking to us?"

He looked at me like I was crazy person. With doubt and a touch of fear in his eyes, he said, "You are the most unusual girl I have ever met."

And so it has gone. I am deeply connected to nature but haven't shared it freely. Until recently.

I've been horse-obsessed my whole life and between the ages of 12 and 26, worked jobs revolving around animals. Even now, I have a deep connection with my cat, Hobbes, and felt it when my husband and I owned two large dogs (two large and VERY needy dogs).

I have a number of friends who are deeply connected to nature, too. One of them, Heather, describes how she goes out and sits with the trees. They teach her things. Sometimes they answer her questions, other times they ask her for help.

For me, recently, the rivers have been speaking to me. They answer a question someone else has asked and I share the answer as a form of guidance. Or I share a realization I have about an event someone had near the water (I interpret, or act as a divine mirror). I also breathe with and for the water and the trees.

Society responds by telling me I'm a crazy person. That I make all this up in my head. "That's a good imagination, right there," I've heard.

Nature tells me, "No. You are not crazy. This is the normal way of the world and you are solidly part of it, connected to it, and communicating through it.

Journal Prompt

What connection do YOU have to nature? What messages, signs, symbols, or conversations have you shared with nature? Is there a practice you could begin that could make this connection stronger, deeper, or truer? What would happen if you started today?

Lessons from a Snail

One weekend, my husband and I loaded our yellow and black Labrador Retrievers into the back of our Subaru and headed out to hike a new-to-us trail near our house in Pisgah Forest. It had been awhile since we'd done a hearty hike and we all desperately needed it (dogs included)!

After choosing a loop hike that we hoped wouldn't be overly crowded, we strapped on our hiking boots, leashed the dogs, and stepped onto the trail.

As we moved away from the road, it grew more and more quiet. We crossed a stream and it immediately got cooler. The smells and sounds of the forest overwhelmed my senses.

At a lower trail junction, we headed to the right and began to climb. Immediately, I could tell this 3.7-mile loop was going to kick my ass. As we progressed, more than half of it was uphill and was pretty steep in places. Switchbacks between rhododendron thickets, small stream crossings that were wet and slippery, plus a few sets of stairs really challenged me.

At one point early on in the hike, after stopping several times to let me catch up, Nelson asked if I wanted him to wait for me. I didn't. Although I was grateful he asked, I knew myself well enough to know I'd feel pressure trying to keep up with him. It's just better for me to hike on my own while still knowing he'd be there, at the end, for me.

Nelson and the dogs hiked ahead while I persevered one step at a time, supported and empowered by my trusty hiking poles. As a side note, hiking with poles has changed how far and fast I can hike. The support and confidence I feel is pretty remarkable. That being said, at one point on a long uphill climb I had my head down, huffing and puffing, wondering why I was doing this to myself. "If I turn around now," I thought, "it's all downhill from here back to the car." I felt tired and alone — and more than a little vulnerable.

And that's when I almost stepped on it. On the trail directly in front of me was a little snail heading *uphill.*

I pondered this little creature, so small and determined. Doing her little snail thing, slowly, but certainly.

Carefully maneuvering around her on the narrow trail, I had the sudden urge to laugh. A huge smile plastered itself across my face. I saw the lesson in the moment: if this small snail can be heading uphill on this trail, carrying everything she has on her back, surely I, with nothing more than a small backpack and a flask of water, can continue uphill, too.

A bit later I passed a black snake sunning on the side of the trail. She (or he) didn't really react as I jumped back with a small squeal. We watched each other for awhile before I continued my upward climb. I arrived at the top, still huffing and puffing, to find Nelson and the dogs resting at the trail junction.

Overall, we had a great day. I'm happy I kept leaning on those hiking poles, going up that mountain one step at a time. I'm happy I didn't quit. As often happens, my hike delivered an unexpected lesson from nature herself. Keep going, even if it's uphill with everything you own on your back.

Journal Prompt

What small lessons does nature teach you when you are paying attention?

Fire

One of the elements of nature that I don't speak about much is fire. I tend to think about fire as a destructive force. Too hot to handle. Potentially uncontrollable.

Where we used to live (in western North Carolina), there were several weeks of forest fires burning thousands of acres during the spring of 2017. The air was choked with smoke and several communities received evacuation warnings. For weeks the fire burned on.

It was a scary time.

My husband and I were never in immediate danger, but we had many in our community who were. We talked about what we'd grab if we had to go. It's an interesting exercise to go through.

One of the other things we talked about was the nature and purpose of fire. Nelson feels the "let it burn" policy is a good one because sending all that effort out to protect life and property is a better use of resources than trying to extinguish a fire in an unoccupied (by humans) forest. With a degree in forestry and as a former wild-land firefighter, he explained that fire is a necessary event for forests. The burning of the underbrush is very beneficial for the trees and it helps prevent much bigger, hotter fires in the future.

And here's the point where I start to feel a little squirrely about fire. I don't want to talk about it for fear of being labeled or misunderstood (or for being accused, again, of having a great imagination).

But, here goes.

While I am an Earth sign (as a Capricorn), I have a lot of fire in me. And it comes out in a such a way that I *feel* it and the people around me feel it.

It happened one day when I was in a business meeting (with a married couple who own a business). We were talking about growing their business and identifying what wasn't working. At some point, one of the two brought up how several of their male employees suddenly felt emboldened to speak offensively about women and minorities. These two business owners shifted uncomfortably in their seats. The husband said,

"I've never directly heard it but if I did, I'd put a stop to it immediately."

The wife said, "They say the worst things about women and minorities while I'm sitting there in the room. It's appalling the things they say."

And I got the feeling. It started swirling in my belly. It rose up through my solar plexus, pierced my heart, and raced out through my voice.

I looked at both of them and said, "I need to put the business talk on hold for a second."

I looked right at the woman and said, "Your responsibility for women and minorities, towards all people really, is to use your voice. You stand up the next time you hear them start saying these offensive things. You look them right in the eyes and say, 'NO. This is unacceptable behavior. Stop this right now.'"

I looked at the husband and requested, "Will you back her up, support her, and keep her safe?"

"Absolutely," he said. "I don't want this happening to my wife, in our company, or anywhere else."

The force of focus and power that came through me wasn't entirely my own. I've felt it many times in the past and it is *intense.* And I realize right now I have only told maybe one or two people EVER about this power of the Divine Feminine Fire that I feel.

She comes through when I'm teaching, and I feel one of my students shrinking from his or her own power. She comes through when I see a man trying to take advantage of a woman (I believe I stopped a rape in my college years because of this). She came through when I almost had a head-on collision with a taxi on a snow-covered road. She comes through when I hear someone who is exhausted and confused and at the end of their rope. And she comes through when I see or hear or read *truth.* And she comes through when I think I can't go on.

Her FIRE is wisdom, compassion, truth telling, and 'stop the bulishit' all wrapped in one.

My FIRE is allowing this to come through me to pierce the right heart at the right time, hopefully in the right way. It has taken me a very long time to realize that this part of me — this fire — is perfectly natural. A part of nature. A part of MY nature.

Nature wants you to recognize that fire isn't bad. It's such a part of the natural world, and because you are part of the natural world, it's a glorious part of you, too.

Journal Prompt

Do you have natural fire in you? How does it show up? For whom does it show up? What does it feel like inside you? What is its purpose? And how do you honor it?

Who else do you know who has the fire? Will you honor them and tell them today that you recognize and honor it in them?

Embrace the Darkness

Exploring a place at night is so completely different than seeing it in the daylight. I have found I am different because my eyes are no longer my primary sense. It's my ears, tongue, skin, and even my intuition that step forward to assist my experience.

There's something about the darkness that scares us — or maybe we've been taught to fear the darkness because of fairy tales, movies, TV, and the news. Bad things happen at night. Bad people are out at night.

And many a parent and grandparent can be heard saying, "Nothing good happens after dark."

I personally have been delighted to discover the magic and mystery of dark.

My husband and I visited Joshua Tree National Park for five days in the fall of 2017. We spent plenty of time exploring nooks and crannies in the park during the daytime, but we also spent time at night exploring different "sights."

For instance, did you know that spider's eyes reflect? They illuminate when your headlamp finds them. It is the coolest thing ever!

Have you ever heard the rustling of something in the bushes and your mind starts screaming, "Bear! Cougar! Something big is coming that is going to eat me!" only to discover it is a cute little armadillo or kangaroo mouse?

Have you ever experienced the night-sounds of coyotes yip-yip-yipping to each other and then letting loose with the most fantastical chorus of howls that echo throughout the night?

And do you really, really understand how many stars there are in the sky?

It is so magical it's hard to put into words.

Nighttime in Joshua Tree National Park gave us these things and more. We were gifted with a coyote sighting (she had a rabbit snack in her mouth as she crossed the road in front of us), watching a meteor blaze across the sky over our camp, and participating in the sunset, seeing the light change from yellow to pink to purple to blue, and ultimately, to black as the stars emerged by the dozens.

One of my best memories from my 2013 Grand Canyon trip was how the night affected me. This excerpt from my book, *Make Some Room: Powerful Life Lessons Inspired by an Epic 16 Day Colorado River Rafting Trip through Grand Canyon* explains it best.

"… And nighttime. Oh, nighttime! As the sun began to set each evening, the heat would lift off our shoulders like some heavy wool blanket we'd toss aside. The colors would wow us to the point where we'd stop our activity to just stare; we were powerless to do anything beyond gazing at the colors while breathing in the cooler evening air. As night descended, the stars made their entrance as a brilliant, twinkling white quilt over our heads. We were dazzled by the sight of it.

Despite not wearing a watch, I seemed to wake up each night around the same time. I'd wiggle around in my sleeping bag, slip on my glasses, and gaze at the Milky Way stretching across the night sky. It was like a divine art show painted each night just for me."

That's how I feel about the night. Not scared but awed at the beauty and majesty. And remember, this happened sleeping on cot on the banks of Colorado, one mile deep in Grand Canyon. There were 15 other people sort of nearby, but this is pretty close to feeling as alone and exposed as I've ever been.

Nature has a suggestion: on the next very dark night, would you consider heading out into the night? Wrap up in a blanket or warm clothes. Sit in the darkness. Meditate if you feel comfortable doing that. If you have a hammock, go lie in it. Listen to the night sounds. "See" in the dark using senses other than your eyes.

If you don't want to head out into the darkness, what about turning off all your lights and electronic devices inside? Let the dark come to you. Use candles to set the mood. Settle in your living room to "see" without lights. Use your other glorious senses.

In the darkness, it could be delightfully playful to consider your relationship with the light.

If you fear the darkness but feel brave enough to head outside, try it one night during a full moon. The illumination might help your fear briefly step aside.

Let the night come. Listen. Feel. Taste. Look. Greet the moon and the stars (because you are literally made of stardust). If you allow it, you'll feel a kinship, a connection. This might expand your ability to feel and sense comfortably without using your eyes.

Settle in for 10, 20, or 30 minutes. No expectations. Just be there, in it. With it. It's a magically different feeling. Become part of the night and let the darkness embrace you.

Journal Prompt

Without the light, how do you feel about the darkness? What stories are you making up about the darkness? In what ways do you honor the light over the darkness? What would need to happen to make the darkness your friend?

About those Miracles

While I was campground hosting in Alaska during the summer of 2018, two miracles happened in one day for me.

One was absolutely from nature and one was a fourth repetition of a message I kept getting during a previous specific week.

Miracle One: I was meditating on the idea of "chop wood and carry water" as I was slinging trash and scrubbing pit toilets (remember that I was working as a campground host). While working, I was thinking, "Gosh, I could be in a bad mood about this work that is neither glamorous nor fun. People could be judging me for doing a job that's *beneath* my skills and talents. Instead, I feel very happy. Peaceful. Calm. Meditative, even. Chop wood and carry water. That's all I am doing right here in this moment." As soon as I completed that train of thought, I looked up to see a bald eagle soar about 10 feet above me.

Miracle Two: One week during the summer of 2018, I kept getting the message to **just show up**. The message came clearly twice one day and an again the next. The following day, I was driving around the campground listening to a podcast while I worked. My signal dropped out at the back of the campground and the recording stopped working. I finished cleaning the final restrooms, returned to the car, and flopped down into the driver's seat. Suddenly, the recording started back and person being interviewed said, "You just have to keep showing up. Do the work and keep showing up."

This kind of stuff happens to me all the time and I freaking LOVE it. The Universe just keeps showing up for me, giving me signs and signals and messages that I cannot explain, but which are so clearly and perfectly obvious. As random as some of the instruction and directions seem, I keep following them.

Journal Prompt

Do you believe in miracles? Signs? Prompts? Messages from the Universe? If so, keep a list of them: do it now! Write them down when they happen so you don't forget. Give thanks for the seen and unseen (but felt) support you receive.

Now follow the instructions you get. They are gifts. Receive them with gratitude and a willing heart.

Magic, Mystery, Wonder

I was on my way to a "Train the Trainer" session for a business foundations class I was teaching. Traffic was heavy, even at 7:30 in the morning. The news on radio was focusing on the weird U.S. election and on atrocities happening overseas.

My hands tightly gripped the steering wheel of my Subaru and I felt myself shift into defensive driving mode. I didn't want to be late and I didn't want to be in an accident. Suddenly, my eyes caught movement on my windshield.

Plop. It was there and then gone.

Plop. There it was again ... and then gone.

Suddenly, lots of tiny plops were appearing on my hood and my windshield.

Snowflakes! The very first of the season for me.

I felt joy well up in my chest. A smile curved my lips upward. I laughed out loud with delight. In this moment of stress and hurry, here was nature giving me a show.

A snow show! My FAVORITE thing ever!

I kept driving and the more westward I went, the more it snowed. I drove past my destination and up the road and up the mountain. It just kept snowing those tiny little snowflakes like crazy.

I pulled into the parking lot of a church. The view was incredible. I sat behind the wheel and watched the snow fall. Beautiful. Gentle. Meditative.

I quietly whispered my thanks to nature, put my car in drive, and headed back down the mountain. I made it to my meeting with a few minutes to spare.

Nature wants to remind you that even in the middle of the hustle and bustle of life we need to be open to the gift of receiving. Receive her beauty. Receive her delight. Receive her joy as it rains down on you.

Journal Prompt

When was the last time you received a gift from nature? Society tells us the cold, the rain, and the snow are a bother. I disagree, for they are the very gifts that remind us we are ALIVE. When was the last time you felt alive in the weather?

Go out in Nature

On social media and in person, I am hearing from many people who are feeling overwhelmed, scared, and angry. There are myriad reasons for this, and I have a solution.

Go out in nature.

Seriously. There's something about nature that helps us be more generous, more trusting, and more helpful towards others.

There's tons of research to back this up. See the Appendix for several well-researched books if you want the numbers and data.

Personally, I think it probably has something to do with the phytoncides I mentioned earlier. It probably also has to do with being still and quiet, and just breathing.

Whatever it is, the solution is to go outside. Sit at the base of a tree. Watch the birds flit about doing their birdie thing. If you can, go find a creek and sit next her. Let her gurgle and laugh until you feel like joining her.

Nature shares with me that she wants you to bring your exhaustion outside to rest with her. She wants you to cry with her waterfalls. She wants you to peel off your socks and shoes and splash in her waters with abandon. And she really wants you to come hug her trees.

Will you give it a try today? Go and sit a spell.

Breathe. Rest Do this only for yourself first.

Then do it so you can re-enter the world with other humans in a mindset that is more generous, more trusting, and more helpful to all of humanity.

A Gift from the River

I believe in magic and miracles. I know I already said this in an earlier chapter. The thing is, I believe because over and over I have the most awesome things happen to me that feel like odd coincidences or divine winks. Some of these things make me laugh out loud. Others leave me standing, mouth gaping, in the wonder of the magic or miracle that just presented itself to me.

A lovely bit of magic happened one Sunday when my hubby, a friend, and I were paddling on the French Broad River near Rosman, North Carolina. We were just a mile or two from the end of the trip, floating along, talking and laughing.

As we floated under a bridge, something colorful caught my eye. "Hey!" I exclaimed. "There's a piece of pottery or something down in the river buried in the sand!"

I turned my boat and paddled upstream against the current. I plunged my arm into the cold water, but the object was just a bit farther than my reach.

My hubby saved the day. He turned his canoe upstream and reached into the water and snagged the vase with his fingers. Pulling the gift from the water he held it up into the light. "There's not a crack on it!" he marveled.

And thus, the river gifted me a vase.

And for a few days, that's all it was. A funny little wonderful gift.
Then, I had lunch with a girlfriend. She and I were discussing the topics of doorways and thresholds and the symbolism of crossing through.

Oddly, just the day before I had stumbled over an email conversation from six years ago with my coach Shannon Presson. She had prompted me to go deeper into something odd that happened during a meditation that had to do with a door.

So, thinking of both the conversation with a friend and the prompt my coach had given me, I decided to dig a little deeper into the significance of this vase that showed up in my life.

What I found gobsmacked me! Turns out, that vase was the perfect metaphor for the changes I'd been experiencing professionally and personally.

Here's what I discovered:

The vase is a universal symbol for the Great Mother. A vase is considered the "feminine receptive" in form and contains the principle life source. It signifies acceptance, receptivity, fertility, and heart. In Hindu, it is Shakti. It's a place where miracles occur. A vase is said to hold the secret of transmutation. From the vase comes nourishment and flowing waters and is a symbol of spiritual abundance.

I will take each and every one of those things. It's like the Great Mother reached out and smacked me on my head. "Pay attention, Darling. Great things are already here if you allow yourself to dig just a bit deeper into the magic and mystery that life presents to you."

I got it. Thanks!

Journal Prompt

When something curious happens, can you dig a little deeper to find the symbolism? Let your fingers do the walking as you type your questions into the search bar on the internet. You, too, could be gobsmacked by what nature is trying to share with you.

Message from the River

One day I was walking barefooted upstream in the Escalante River in Utah. My husband and I had hiked the sandy trails to Natural Bridge — the ancient sandstone arch that had been worn away by wind and water. We spent several hours in the shade of the bridge, tucked up in the sandy alcove high above the trail.

As we began to venture home, the heat of the afternoon was a clear invitation to slip off our shoes and start walking in the river. The cool, clear water flowed over my feet and around my ankles. I walked with care, avoiding rocks, and advancing through sand bars.

We spotted all sorts of animal tracks, from birds, to river otters, to mule deer. Following a bend in the river, I placed my feet once, twice, and a third time. Then, I got stuck.

I tried moving my foot to the left. Nope, too many rocks. I tried moving my foot right. OUCH! I'd placed the tender ball of my foot on a particularly sharp rock that time.

I stopped and evaluated my situation. I didn't see how I could move forward. The areas both left and right of me were very rocky and I knew I couldn't progress without some serious pain.

Suddenly, a suggestion appeared in my mind, given to me by the river: *Go backward.* What? Oh right! A direction I hadn't thought of was to go back the way I came. Duh!

So, with the river's help, I carefully moved back the way I'd come about four or five feet. Once there, I could clearly see a path off to the right where I could follow the sandy bottom and avoid the rocky shoals, a path I'd missed before.

I gave a silent prayer of thanks, and we continued up the river.

Journal Prompt

When you are stuck, nature can provide unexpected answers. What answers have you received recently from nature? If you haven't ever thought about this, let now be the time.

River Magic

In 2016, when my husband and I rafted all 149 miles of the French Broad River from Rosman, NC to Newport, TN in 13 days, we were mostly unsupported. We experienced tons of river magic from terrific people, but no one gave us more help than a guy we met in Asheville named DaveWave.

DaveWave and his wife own Asheville Outdoor Center. They offer river trips to anyone wants to enjoy the lovely French Broad River.

We met DaveWave when we wandered over from our stop at the Wilson RV Center where we were camping for the night. We'd heard a rumor that the Asheville Outdoor Center had put in a small bar.

Indeed, we found what we were looking for and DaveWave cheerfully served us a cider and a beer. We got talking and explained to him we were rafting the whole river.

"No kidding!" he said. "That is so cool, and these beers are officially on the house. What do you guys need?"

He asked us that question a couple times. Finally, we confessed we needed help with a shuttle between the two lower dams. We had already self-portaged our 800 pounds of gear over and around the first dam and it was a total bitch. The next two dams (only two miles apart) were going to be much more difficult. Steep embankments on private property — and did I mention there were *two* of them?

DaveWave said immediately, "I got you. What day do you need help, where, and what time? I'll bring my truck and open trailer."

With that settled, and with our profuse thanks, he offered to show us around his set up at the center. He showed us some photos, their gear, their awesome patio, and his art.

Oh my gosh. His art.

DaveWave is a passionate outdoorsman, but at heart he is an artist. Some of things he's done with wood and metal would blow your mind. I wish I had photos to share!

As he was talking, he casually mentioned he takes wood from the river for some of his projects. "I don't know if I should," he said, almost confessing. "And I don't know how much is too much."

Suddenly, I found myself answering, "Just ask. The river just told me that you should ask. It will let you know when you are about to take too much."

DaveWave looked at me with just a little bit of side eye. "Okay," he said. "I'll ask."

And just like that, I learned the rivers will communicate with me. Through me. Sometimes the message is for me. Sometimes it's meant for someone else.

It's a deep honor for me to be able to hear the rivers speak. And it makes me curious — do you hear the rivers speak?

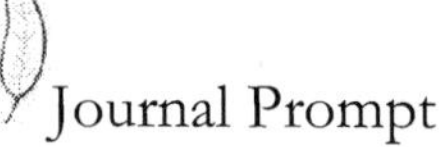

Journal Prompt

Have you ever received a message from the river? An urge to speak an answer to a question? If you haven't received one, would you feel open enough to receive one? Why or why not?

Go with the Flow

I have rafted and kayaked thousands of miles. As a family, we rafted the American River in Sacramento, CA each summer. In college, I took canoeing as part of my PE credit courses. And in the late 90's, my brother and sister-in-law gave me my first kayak. Best. Present. Ever. I was hooked and have kayaked with a joy bordering on obsession ever since.

It was taking a few extended whitewater rafting trips with my husband, though, that taught me some real lessons about being like water and learning to go with the flow.

In my book, *Make Some Room: Powerful Life Lessons Inspired an Epic 16-day Colorado River Rafting Trip Through Grand Canyon,* I learned how to be bold and brave 14-seconds at a time as we ran the mighty Colorado River. That rafting trip through Grand Canyon was *hard.* It was work. The rapids were bigger than anything I had ever imagined. Those rapids helped me learn to conquer my fear of whitewater. I still have enormous respect for it, but I am no longer mind-numbingly terrified.

In 2016, my husband and I completed a trip of the entire French Broad River, which begins in Rosman, North Carolina and ends at Lake Douglas in Tennessee. It took us 13 days and we were self-supported through the entire 149 miles. On that trip, my husband taught me a lot about reading the water. More often than not, he'd say, "Just watch where the main and biggest flow of the water goes. Let the river carry the raft and don't fight it. Just go with the flow."

You don't need to do an epic whitewater trip to see the flow. Next time it rains, go outside and watch the water flow down your driveway. See where it goes and why. Connect with the fluidity and simplicity. It's the same in your body. It can be the same in your life.

When you don't fight what wants to happen, life can carry you sweetly along.

Journal Prompt

In what areas of your life can you sense what wants to happen? Can you release your death-grip on the shore and soar out into the current? Can you let the momentum take you where it will?

Messages of Healing

My friend Jeni shared this experience with me after she experienced healing by visiting with the trees. Here's the gift she was given:

"I went to a parole hearing one morning and I had been pondering the question of trust. The board had asked this man what his plans were for learning to trust and to be trusted (as this was defined as one of his failures in the past). I had no answer myself. I left there thinking how on earth would you define that path enough to articulate a plan for it?

So I went for a walk to my favorite tree. This tree often provides me with gifts and insights because it prompts me to be still. This day, the sun was shining, and it was beautiful outside.

When I got to the tree, they invited me to sit on one of their roots. I did and I noticed a hummingbird flitting around. I sat there longer; a jogger went past. I sat some more; my bum went noticeably numb, still I didn't move, waiting. I didn't know for what.

And then it happened. The birdsong came back. I knew then that my presence had been the reason it had stopped but I had sat still so long, they began to sing again. I had trusted the tree to guide me to stillness that lasted long enough for the birds to trust me. Then the magic was revealed in all of their songs, by the flicker of all their movements, and by the hummingbird that landed nearby, his ruby head highlighted perfectly by the bright sunshine.

So, I thought, perhaps that is what I was seeking. You must trust to be trusted. It cannot go only one way. I realized that no matter how many times I go to sit there, it might take time for the bird trust to reveal the music.

The gift may be different every time. I may always have to wait. But each time I might find it easier to know that the reward is worth it."

Journal Prompt

What questions are you wrestling with right now? Name them by writing them down. Take them out to nature with you. Sit at the base of the trees or on the bank of a river. Get still. Breathe. Ask for guidance.

The Flirting Rock

During the summer of 2017, my husband and I lived and worked at the Trail River Campground, in the Chugach National Forest on the Kenai Peninsula, in Moose Pass, Alaska. We basically lived in a national forest for the summer working as campground hosts (it is and isn't as glamorous as it sounds).

Often, we would walk down to the shores of the Kenai Lake. Sometimes we'd hike around, other days we'd just sit and enjoy the turquoise-green glory that is Kenai Lake.

One day while stomping around, my husband (who is a landscape and nature photographer) stopped in front of a good-sized boulder on the lakeshore and said, "Now, this scenery is pretty, but if I include this big boulder in the shot, it will make the picture really spectacular."

As I focused on the rock, I realized the rock was preening with glee that my husband had noticed it. I mean seriously, the rock was practically *swooning* over my husband's attention of it.

Of course, I shared this information with my husband and told him how very, very pleased the rock was that he had taken notice of it and that it would be very, very happy to be featured is his landscape photo of Kenai Lake and the mountains beyond.

"That rock is totally flirting with you," I said.

This, gentle reader, is the first time I have experienced a communication with a rock. I was startled at first and then just delighted to feel its joy. And mind you, I wasn't even trying to communicate with it (him? the feeling of the rock was rather masculine). I was just standing there trying to be politely interested as my husband waxed poetically about framing up a good photo.

This was the single coolest experience of my time in Alaska.

Journal Prompt

Are you open enough to receive feelings, visions, and thoughts from the natural world? Does the idea scare you, excite you, confuse you?

What does your life story tell you about communicating this way?

Weather

I am a bit obsessed with the weather. I don't much care what's it is doing, but I do like to watch it happen.

Is there a storm coming? You'll find me out on the porch or pressed up against a window waiting and watching.

There's snow in the forecast? I am almost beside myself with joy. And distracted, watching and waiting.

I love the motorhome we purchased because it has a gigantic windshield — it's one big curved piece of glass. There is so much potential looking out that windshield!

In our world of climate-controlled comfort, there's something magical about watching the weather turn. Experiencing it. Being in it. Feeling it get hotter, colder, windier, rainier.

Only twice has the weather come far too close for comfort. Once when I was sleeping outside in a tent during a very violent lightening storm and once in

2016 when my husband and I outran a tornado on a highway in Kansas.

But other weather? Give me the right gear and stick me out in it. I'm one happy camper!

How about you? Is there a particular kind of weather you adore? It's okay if it's the return of heat and humidity or if it's worshipping the white stuff that falls from the sky in winter.

Whatever the weather, how will you notice and appreciate what is happening in the moment?

Journal Prompt

Whatever the weather, go outside right now and stand it in. Focus on how your skin feels. Taste the weather by sticking out your tongue. How does the weather sound? What do you see? What do you sense is happening *around* you? What do you sense is now happening *within* you?

Desert Magic

During one of my hikes in Joshua Tree National Park this past October, I was walking along asking Mother Earth, the Universe, etc. what to do about some gifts and talents I'm not using because I'm afraid.

I'm standing on top of a mountain and the wind is blowing like crazy. Clouds are zipping by and the sun plays peekaboo with them. There's no one else up there except me and Nelson and he's "over there" somewhere taking photos.

I go still and quiet and ask for help from my guides and allies (like my gloriously wise friend Fen suggests).

As I turn around, I see this Joshua tree with something at the base. I get closer, and sure enough, a heart lies right there, at the base of the tree.

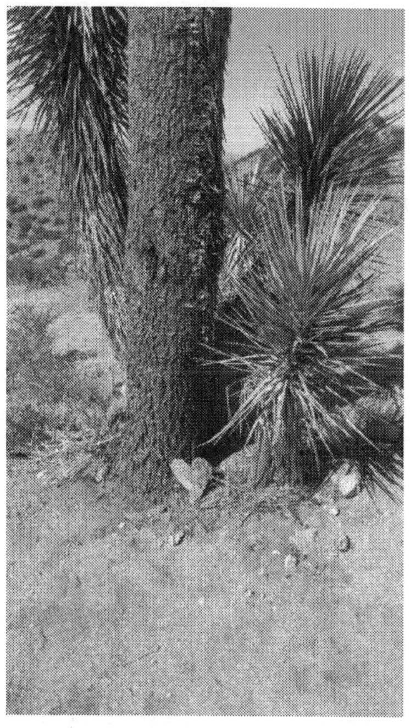

Surely this is the answer I'm seeking, to move into my heart-space. To trust I am supported at all times, in all places.

And that is the love note I want to share with you — trust that you are supported at all times, in all places. It is safe to move into your heart-space and rest there.

Journal Prompt

When you are in nature, how can you practice receiving messages and gifts?

Star Blessing

My Facebook friend, Allison, posted about a magical star blessing she received early one morning. She gave me permission to share her story with you.

She described what happened like this:

"Sometimes, I think we made a mistake living so far out [she recently moved out of the city] but then I take the dogs out for their early morning pee and I see the starry sky. And I know I'm right where I need to be. It called me forward from under the patio, out into the grass. I dug my feet in and raised my arms to let the stars give me their blessing. Heaven on earth at 5:30am."

I adore Allison's description of her star blessing for so many reasons.

We talked about her experience with the morning stars on her Facebook page. She told me that at first, she really resisted going outside that morning. She really wanted to let the dogs out alone to do their thing, but *something* called her forward.

Because she listened to the call and looked up, she noticed how amazing the sky looked. Then, she heard her body ask her to remove her shoes and get grounded in a mini-Earthing session by stepping barefoot into the grass.

Finally, she heard the invitation of the blessing. As she lifted her arms towards the sky, she received the blessing from the stars.

Heaven on earth at 5:30 in the morning, indeed.

Life is simply magical when we pay attention.

Journal Prompt

Is there a call from nature you've received recently? Did you answer it or push it away? Next time, what will you do?

Seeing with New Eyes

While we were boondocking in the middle of the Coconino Forest outside Flagstaff, Arizona, I spent a lot of time in meditation. My hubby spent a lot of time taking gorgeous photos.

What I love is when a photo captures a miracle — a note from nature — and it isn't *seen* until it is *noticed*.

What am I saying here?

My husband took this photo of our kitty Hobbes as he was sitting on the dash of our motorhome one morning.

Nelson was simply taking another beautiful photo. He didn't see what was there until after he took the photo.

He didn't notice the miracle until he recognized it.

I've found noticing these small miracle moments take awareness and practice.

Journal Prompt

Gentle reader, what are you not seeing or not noticing?

How can you slow down and begin noticing the small miracles right in front of you?

Allow Your Heart to Feel

When I sit among the trees, or in the grass, or sometimes even floating on the water in my kayak, weeping is a refreshment. This moving of emotion matters to me. When I weep, I come clean.

There are some poets who pierce my heart with their words. When I sit, and read of their sorrows, their longings, and their open-heartedness, I often sit and weep.

Some poets move me like no one else. I particularly love Mary Oliver, David Whyte, and Rumi. Something about their storytelling and the cadence of words shreds me open. Allowing daylight in and emotion out.

This week, I read the following poem from Rumi.

Before you read it, I have a recommendation…
Take this outside with you. Find someplace quiet. Be alone.

Read this poem out loud to your heart. To your Soul. In dedication of your Spirit.

Read it out loud. Let the words moisten your mouth.
Let them parch your thirst.

Let the words be a love song, a healing song, you sing
to yourself.

Read this poem out loud to your whole Divine Being.

Sorrow prepares you for joy.
It violently sweeps everything out of your house,
so that new joy can find space to enter.
It shakes the yellow leaves from the bough of your heart,
so that fresh, green leaves can grow in their place.
It pulls up the rotten roots,
so that new roots hidden beneath have room to grow.
Whatever sorrow shakes from your heart,
far better things will take their place.

~ Jalal al-Din Muhammad Rumi

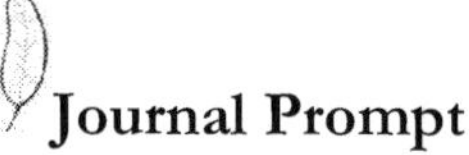

Journal Prompt

For the poem above, substitute "me/my" everywhere you see the word "you/your" in the poem. Read it out loud again with those substitutions. Indeed, this will magnify and personalize these words like nothing else.

Write down the differences you feel (thoughts, feelings, emotions).

Just Wander

In 2017, my husband and I took a subcontracting job that had us living in our motorhome in parking lots of strip malls.

One weekend, we decided to get off the concrete and reserved two nights at the Chattahoochee Bend State Park in Georgia. It was time to just wander in nature.

This state park had a number of nice, easy trails and we took advantage of the time among the trees. Since the hiking wasn't strenuous, there was plenty of time for meandering, pondering, and wandering.

Without a real destination, it's lovely to wander and just see what catches your eye.

At one point, I spotted some brilliant red leaves among the dormant browns and muted greens. A few mushrooms hung out. And there were many heart-shaped leaves scattered alongside the trail. I didn't care about the genus or species of the plants. I just enjoyed seeing them.

When I found some bones, I didn't wonder too hard what kind of animal they came from. I just enjoyed inspecting them. And when I found a log to sit and meditate on, I made lovely use of it.

Your brain and nervous system will thank you. Wandering in nature stabilizes your hormones and improves your breathing. In fact, the trees emit essential oils that you breathe in that help boost your immunity.

While all that science stuff is great (it really IS), just the act of wandering is good for your soul.

All this is to simply encourage you to find time to wander. Whether you do it in your backyard or a park, it doesn't matter.

Journal Prompt

When was the last time you simply wandered in nature?

Come Alive

There's a well-known quote by Gil Bailie, founder and president of The Cornerstone Forum, where he requests that we all figure out what makes us come alive. He insists that is what the world needs. I cannot argue with him.

I love Gil Bailie's sentiment because he doesn't ask us to do anything for anyone else. He simply invites us to go *inward* and figure out what makes us feel *alive*. Then he gives us permission to go out and do that because it's actually what the world needs.

Someone in my life who is the epitome of someone who practices his passion is my brother Steve.

This is a man who lives to fish. He loves to fish. He will forgo sleep, suffer through the rain, and endure the cold to go out and fish. He will drive miles to fish for a few hours. He takes friends and family out fishing. Or he'll go alone if he can't find anyone to join him, but he finds joy in sharing his passion with others — he's the extrovert in our family.

The more he fishes, the happier he is.

And when he fishes, he takes beautiful photos of sunrises and sunsets. He gets fabulous photos of rivers, lakes, and the oceans he fishes on. He spends time outside enjoying the birds, deer, raccoons, and other animals he sees while on those waters.

He's never said so, but I'd bet nature speaks to him while he's out there.

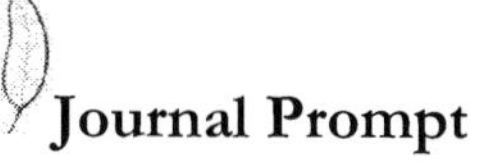 **Journal Prompt**

Let my brother be your role model for practicing a passion. If you know yours, do you eat, sleep, and breathe it?

Go back and re-read the quote for this note. Now is your time to figure out what makes *you* come alive. Go do that.

The world desperately needs people who have come alive!

Close encounters

One day in Joshua Tree National Park, my hubby and I drove the Geology Road, a sandy, dusty 17 miles of 4x4 only single-lane road through a remote part of the park.

As we drove our small 4x4 Chevy Tracker — we named it Bob — along the sandy road, we'd regularly see something worth stopping for.

One time was a huge set of boulders and an earthen dam constructed by cattlemen who tried to homestead the area.

Another time, Nelson spotted some abandoned mines and hiked up to check them out. On his hike down, he found an arrowhead (we left it there and alerted the rangers of its location).

Next was a sharp turn that took us up the road to an overlook that allowed us to see the entire valley we'd just driven. Here, we both got out to stretch our legs and admire the view. Nelson wandered off, camera in hand, and I sat on a big rock to enjoy the scenery. As I sat there, a small bit of movement caught my attention.

Zip. Wiggle. Zip. Wiggle. Zooooooom.

A small white-tailed antelope squirrel was making himself busy looking for scraps.

I spied peanut shells on the ground and figured this little guy was used to getting a handout from tourists. I am not big on feeding the wildlife in wild places, so I just put on my patience hat and watched him. Soon enough, he stopped to watch me. Then he started doing his dance. He'd advance and retreat.

Advance and retreat.

I never moved, but something would happen to freak him out and *zip* he was gone again. Then he would muster his courage and come back.

Finally, he got brave enough to come up next to my knee.

He looked me over, decided I didn't actually have a treat for him (sorry, buddy), then he was on his way to do something that was, hopefully, more productive than begging from me!

I thoroughly enjoyed the interaction. Just sitting, watching him scuffle around, running between, around, and under the rocks, stopping to furiously scratch an itch or pausing to clean his whiskers.

He was so darn cute and I was grateful for the time with him (or her).

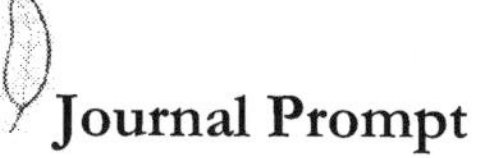

Journal Prompt

Ready to have a close encounter with something wild? I find the birds and squirrels of the suburbs are usually willing.

Go into your backyard armed with birdseed or nuts. Spread them around and then just sit still. Eventually, you'll become part of the background. They'll forget you are there and venture forward.

Enjoy the time observing their fur or feathers, how they move, their crazy breathing, and when they meet your eye.

Go out with patience in your heart. You'll soon find yourself lost in a wild interaction.

Live, Laugh, Love

This note from nature couldn't be any clearer! It arrived as I stepped out of the car at Skull Rock in Joshua Tree National Park.

Someone had left this mat on the sidewalk. I saw it and just smiled.

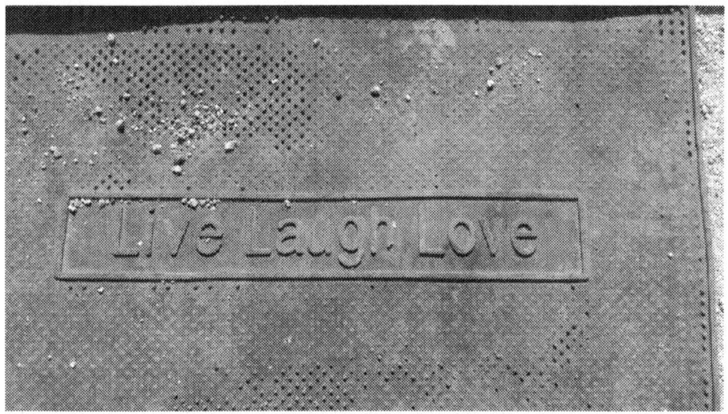

The message is so beautifully simple: Live Laugh Love

I wonder how many people got out of their cars and walked right on past the mat. They never noticed how nature was trying to get their attention with such a simple expression of joy.

Journal Prompt

Look at the world with curious eyes today, gentle reader. What wonderful note from nature did you notice today?

Get Lost

My husband and I make a practice of getting lost. We regularly check out side roads and dirt roads, often not knowing where they lead.

One fine day we were exploring a dirt road in Escalante, Utah. Bumping down through the sand and rocks, Nelson spotted four hoodoos out in the distance. "Let's check them out," he said, grinning.

We drove until there was no more road, parked the car and continued on foot to the four sandstone hoodoo rock formations. As we walked up to them, I uttered something not suitable for print here.

Just beyond the hoodoos, the rock dropped off sharply hundreds of feet to the canyon floor below. Ahead of us, we could see clear across the area known as Escalante Grand Staircase National Monument.

We were *wowed* in every sense of the word.

Our feeling of wow multiplied as the wind picked up and a storm came barreling in behind us.

Pea-sized hail pelted our heads and shoulders as we ran for cover under the sandstone formations.

Luckily the storm skirted to the right of us and the hail stopped. We sat on the edge of the canyon and watched the storm roll and tumble across the land. Curtains of rain covered the desert. Dark clouds gave way to sunshine, which created unbelievable rainbows all around us.

Some days in nature provide more excitement than we could plan for. Our curiosity paid off big time this particular day.

Journal Prompt

Gentle reader: when was the last time you set out for a day of wandering, with no purpose except to see where the road or trail leads you?

Magic, mystery, and wonder await. Go on, get wowed!

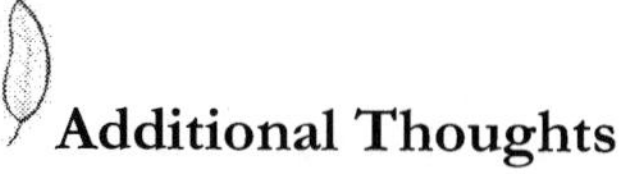

Additional Thoughts

Additional Thoughts

Additional Thoughts

Additional Thoughts

Your Turn

Gentle reader, thank you for purchasing this book.

I hope the stories have been inspirational and thought-provoking for you. Most of all, I hope you've used the exercises to gently nurture your relationship with the natural world to tune into your inner voice.

The whole point of this book to remind you that *you* are part of nature. When you nurture your relationship with the natural world, you are nurturing your relationship with yourself.

Allow yourself to be heard. Allow yourself to be healed.

As you heal yourself, you heal the world.

Journal Prompt

What does your heart long for? How will you satisfy that longing?

Appendix

Book Recommendations

I'm including fiction and non-fiction in my picks because I adored *each* of these books. They gently opened my mind and my heart.

Finding Your Way in a Wild New World by Martha Beck (non-fiction)

Soulcraft by Bill Plotkin (non-fiction)

Affluence without Abundance by James Suzman (non-fiction)

The Overstory by Richard Powers (fiction)

Reclaiming the Wild Soul by Mary Reynolds Thompson (non-fiction)

Diana, Herself by Martha Beck (fiction)

The Nature Fix by Florence Williams (non-fiction)

The Hidden Life of Trees by Peter Wohllenben (non-fiction)

Please be Kind — Review this Book

Thanks for purchasing this book. If you enjoyed it and found the contents useful, please leave a review on Amazon! Your feedback matters!

Acknowledgments

I want to thank my beta readers who found the time to read and give feedback. Jim and Brenda Mattson (always), Warren Williams, Heathir McElroy, Maureen Stoudt, and Celine Landauer Allen. I am also grateful to people who contributed their stories to the 31 Notes from Nature FB group which also ended up as part of this book: Jeni Luther, Fen Druadin Head, Sandra Trca, and Allison Crow.

About the Author

Angie Mattson Stegall is an Executive Wayfinder who guides her clients out of overwork, overwhelm, and burnout. As a "Wayfinder," Angie helps her clients find their own internal map and compass, which naturally leads them to experience true fulfillment, personally and professionally.

Angie earned a BA in Organizational Communications from Queens University of Charlotte and is a Martha Beck Certified Wayfinder Life Coach. She will readily tell you she does her best work with clients when they are outside, barefoot, in the forest. She's in training to become a Certified Forest Therapy Guide through the ANFT.

In business since 2003, Angie shares her extensive entrepreneurship experience through seminars, teaching, and speaking (including classes, breakouts, and keynotes). She's spoken to groups at BlueCross BlueShield of NC, MassMutual Insurance in North and South Carolina, at the Western Women's Business Center's Annual Conference, Duke Energy, FemCity, Sisters United, and eWomen. She's worked with executives and their teams at Duke Energy, MassMutual NC and SC, Doosan, Kuebler Inc., and Corning as well as with dozens of small business owners and their teams.

As a five-time published author, Angie won the 2014 Women's Business Award (author category) at the fifth annual Women's Business Conference and was a Founding Member of the Brevard Authors Guild. She also received the coveted "5 Star Award" in the 2016 Authors Talk About It independent book awards for her fourth book, *Make Some Room: Powerful Life Lessons Inspired by an Epic 16 day Colorado River Rafting Trip through Grand Canyon.*

Angie also offers immersive retreats several times a year with her co-facilitators, Molly Barker, founder of the Girls on the Run International and an Ashoka Fellow, and backpacking retreats with Jayne Fought, lead guide with Island Ford Adventures, based in Brevard, North Carolina.

Personally, Angie and her husband Nelson live to travel and love immersive experiences, like taking a private 16-day Colorado River rafting trip through Grand Canyon and spending 13 days on a self-supported rafting adventure covering all 149 miles of the French Broad River from North Carolina into Tennessee. In 2017, she and her husband sold everything they owned and bought a motorhome. After 25,000 miles of driving throughout the USA, Canada, and visiting Alaska, they've temporarily settled in Gastonia, North Carolina for a new adventure:

caring for Nelson's 85-year-old mother who has Alzheimer's Disease.

Speaking, Workshops, Retreats:

If you're interested in working with Angie or having her speak to your group about any topics related to her books, please feel free to contact her directly at Angie@AngieStegall.com or fill out the Contact form on her website at: AngieStegall.com.

Connect with Angie Mattson Stegall

Facebook AngieStegallWayfinder
LinkedIn: AngelaMattsonStegall
Twitter @angiemstegall
Websites
AngieStegall.com and YukonandBean.com

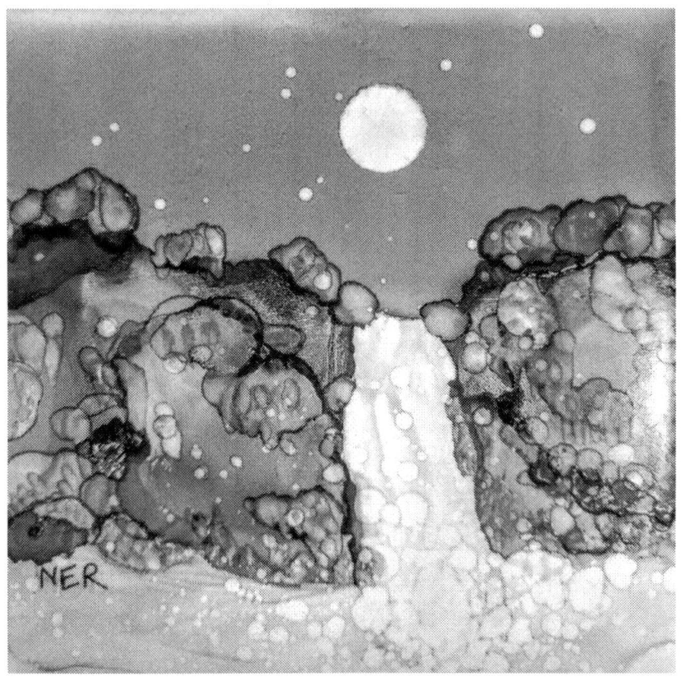

Cover art tile by Nancy E. Richards

To view and purchase more of her stunning artwork, visit: Nancyerichards-artist.com

Made in the USA
Columbia, SC
24 September 2024

42937649R00120